Teaching Ambitiously in Elementary School

Teaching Ambitiously in Elementary School

Preparing Beginning Teachers

PETER YOUNGS AND DOROTHEA ANAGNOSTOPOULOS
WITH JILLIAN M. CAVANNA, COREY DRAKE, TUTITA M. CASA

HARVARD EDUCATION PRESS
CAMBRIDGE, MASSACHUSETTS

Paperback ISBN 9798895570272

Library of Congress Cataloging-in-Publication Data

Names: Youngs, Peter, author. | Anagnostopoulos, Dorothea, author. | Cavanna, Jillian M., author. | Drake, Corey, author. | Casa, Tutita Maria, author.
Title: Teaching ambitiously in elementary school : preparing beginning teachers / Peter Youngs, Dorothea Anagnostopoulos, Jillian M. Cavanna, Corey Drake, Tutita M. Casa.
Description: Cambridge, Massachusetts : Harvard Education Press, [2026] | Includes bibliographical references and index. | Summary: "A richly researched guide to the core competencies and wraparound supports required for quality, ambitious instruction. Through targeted assignments, tailored support, and skillful feedback, ambitious teaching promotes deep, conceptual learning, even at the elementary school level. To help beginning teachers excel at this increasingly in-demand-and demanding-practice, Peter Youngs, Dorothea Anagnostopoulos, Jillian M. Cavanna, Corey Drake, and Tutita M. Casa thoroughly evaluate, in Teaching Ambitiously in Elementary School, the core knowledge and supports necessary for teaching ambitiously across a range of school contexts. The authors draw their insights from an extensive, mixed-methods study involving more than one thousand hours of classroom practice in nearly seventy US school districts. They examine how five elementary teacher preparation programs help beginning teachers develop their craft in pre-service preparation and then enact ambitious instruction in mathematics and English language arts. Considering multiple aspects, including individual teachers' characteristics, goals, and beliefs; the learning opportunities and resources available to them; and their strategies for teaching diverse students, the authors draw an explicit link between learning opportunities during pre-service preparation and the early pedagogy of elementary teachers. They also stress the critical importance of mentoring, coaching, professional training, and effective classroom management in supporting ambitious teaching practice. An essential reference for preservice teachers, practitioners, and researchers focused on qualitative assessments of teacher preparation and practice, Teaching Ambitiously in Elementary School makes a key contribution to enriching the ecosystem in which ambitious teachers can thrive when they first enter the profession"—Provided by publisher.
Identifiers: LCCN 2025020106 | ISBN 9798895570272 (paperback)
Subjects: LCSH: Teachers—Training of—United States. | Education, Elementary—United States.
Classification: LCC LB1715 .Y68 2026
LC record available at https://lccn.loc.gov/2025020106

Published by Harvard Education Press, an imprint of the Harvard Education Publishing Group

Harvard Education Press
8 Story Street
Cambridge, MA 02138

Cover Design: Jackie Shepherd Design
Cover Image: Tanya Syrytsyna via Shutterstock

The typefaces in this book are Adobe Garamond Pro and Myriad Pro.

This book is dedicated to all the beginning elementary teachers who are working tirelessly to foster their students' learning and to the teacher educators and school colleagues supporting them.

Contents

Contents

CHAPTER 1

The Challenges of Preparing Ambitious Beginning Teachers

Efforts to raise learning standards and increase accountability in educational systems in the United States have cast unprecedented attention on teacher quality. Rigorous learning goals, such as those delineated in the Common Core State Standards, emphasize the need for all students, especially students whom the nation's public schools have historically underserved, to develop knowledge of core disciplinary concepts and practices as they engage in inquiry, reasoning, and argumentation. Meeting these goals requires teachers, including those just beginning their careers, to teach ambitiously.

Ambitious instruction is associated with student achievement in multiple subjects and with meeting students' diverse learning needs.[1] Yet teaching ambitiously poses several challenges even for experienced teachers.[2] It requires that teachers skillfully plan for and facilitate students' interactions with disciplinary knowledge in ways that are consistently rigorous; responsive to students' ideas, learning needs, and identities; adaptive to in-the-moment contingencies of teaching and learning; and supportive of more equitable learning outcomes for students who have been historically marginalized because of their race, gender, language, and socioeconomic status.[3] Ambitious instruction can be particularly challenging for beginning elementary teachers, who must establish their competence teaching multiple subjects as they encounter for the first time the full range of teachers' responsibilities to their students, colleagues, and broader communities.

The expectations that beginning teachers teach ambitiously from day one has placed increased scrutiny on the programs that prepare them, especially those programs located in colleges and universities. These programs have been critiqued for failing to prepare novices for the complex realities of the nation's increasingly diverse classrooms.[4] Policy makers have increased regulations regarding college- and university-based preparation programs, with the stated aim of raising their quality. At the same time, policy makers have also supported the creation of alternative routes into teaching that promise easy entry to certification with minimal coursework, reduced time commitments for teacher candidates, and minimal expenditures for states or school districts.[5] Such promises hold particular appeal for underresourced districts that face continued teacher shortages and that are more likely to serve racially and linguistically diverse students and students living in poverty.[6] As the diversity of students enrolled in the nation's schools has increased,[7] the teacher preparation landscape has become increasingly complex, making it both more imperative and more challenging to ensure that novice teachers receive the learning opportunities and resources they need to teach all students ambitiously.

This book addresses this imperative. Drawing on findings from the Development of Ambitious Instruction (DAI) study, a research study in which we followed 175 elementary teachers from five different university-based teacher preparation programs into their first years of teaching, we explore the learning opportunities and resources that help beginning teachers teach ambitiously. We focus on novice elementary teachers, given the long tail of their potential effects on student learning and life outcomes. Having a skillful elementary teacher can positively shape students' future educational opportunities and outcomes as well as workforce opportunities and earnings.[8] The learning experiences and supports in teacher preparation programs and elementary schools that assist beginning elementary teachers in building ambitious teaching practices can thus serve as key levers for improving important student outcomes.

While identifying these experiences and supports is critical, it is equally critical that we understand *how* they help beginning teachers enact ambitious instruction. Doing so requires that we consider how individual novice teachers' goals, actions, and characteristics (e.g., prior experiences, knowledge, self-efficacy, and identity) interact with their learning opportunities and access to resources available in teacher preparation and elementary school settings to shape their instruction. In other words, it is not sufficient for preparation programs or districts to provide courses, field placements, and instructional coaches with certain features, qualities, and resources. Instead, preparation and induction programs must also take into account the ways in which beginning teachers' goals, actions, and characteristics shape their learning and development of ambitious practices in the various contexts in which they build their teaching practice.

In this chapter, we first define ambitious instruction and briefly summarize what current research tells us about how beginning teachers learn to enact it. Much of this research focuses either on how small numbers of novices learn to teach ambitiously in a single subject or on measuring the effects of particular aspects of teacher preparation on preK–12 student achievement outcomes. Critical questions remain about the opportunities to learn in teacher preparation that enable beginning teachers across multiple programs and diverse elementary school settings to enact ambitious instruction in their first years of teaching. Questions about potential subject matter differences are also salient for elementary teachers, who typically teach multiple subjects. In addition, since novice teachers must learn to use the curricular and instructional resources available in the schools where they begin their careers, further insight is needed into how these resources shape whether and how early career teachers develop ambitious teaching practices. We then describe the DAI study and how it addresses these current gaps in our understanding of how to prepare beginning teachers to teach ambitiously. We conclude with an overview of subsequent chapters.

AMBITIOUS INSTRUCTION

Ambitious instruction promotes students' deep, conceptual understanding of academic content. It is evident in the tasks teachers select, the ways teachers support students in engaging in those tasks, and the ways in which teachers respond to what students think and do.[9] Ambitious instruction provides students opportunities to participate in reasoning and argumentation and to actively make sense of academic tasks as they develop such disciplinary practices as comparing solution methods in mathematics, considering one's audience when writing texts, and studying the natural world and then proving explanations based on evidence.[10] Teachers who teach ambitiously focus students on the intellectual processes that support them in completing demanding tasks. This includes prompting students to justify their approaches to tasks, elaborate on their explanations, and clarify their thinking.

In an elementary English language arts (ELA) lesson, for example, ambitious instruction would include the teacher talking with students about why readers might focus on making inferences from information in a text. The teacher would also model one way to evaluate text information or draw conclusions from it and explain why and how to use it. As the students engage with the text, the teacher encourages them to make, compare, elaborate, and clarify their own and their classmates' inferences and interpretations.[11] Throughout the lesson, the teacher positions students as capable of engaging in meaningful disciplinary work while maintaining rigor, providing instructional scaffolding, and making disciplinary practices explicit in ways that support all learners.[12]

In an elementary mathematics lesson where the class is assigned word problems, for another example, teaching ambitiously would include the teacher viewing each child as a mathematician who is able to determine appropriate mathematical procedures for addressing various concepts embodied within the word problems. Rather than have students merely apply such procedures, the teacher would highlight why mathematicians and others might determine their own approaches and want to analyze and compare different procedures. As they engage with a range of problem-solving tasks, the teacher might support students by providing manipulatives and/or visual models and encourage students to share and justify multiple solution strategies, use multiple representations, and explore connections among them.[13] A key element of ambitious instruction is, again, the balance among the disciplinary demand of the task; the foregrounding of students' ideas, thinking, and funds of knowledge; and the teacher's provision of instructional scaffolding to support meaningful intellectual work.

A growing body of studies, typically employing qualitative research methods, examine beginning teachers' development of ambitious instruction. Many of these studies explore how preservice teachers learn to enact ambitious teaching practices as they examine representations of ambitious practices, identify their component parts, and rehearse employing them in increasingly complex settings.[14] Other studies follow novices from preservice preparation to in-service teaching to document whether and how they enact the ambitious instructional practices they encountered in teacher preparation.[15] Some of these studies describe how beginning teachers variously frame learning goals in relation to understanding authentic texts, real-world phenomena, and central disciplinary ideas; elicit and expand on students' ideas; and press students for evidence-based explanations.[16] These studies provide "existence proofs" that novices can enact ambitious teaching practices. At the same time, they also indicate that novice teachers often enact ambitious practices only partially or eschew them entirely as they adopt conventional teacher-centered practices focused more on recall and rote learning endorsed by school colleagues and/or policies.[17]

While these studies provide rich portraits of both teacher education pedagogies and beginning teachers' development of ambitious instruction, they typically include small numbers of teachers and preparation programs, and they often focus on a single subject area and one or two instructional practices. This leaves unanswered questions about how novice teachers develop a broader range of ambitious practices across subject areas. Questions also remain concerning the types of learning opportunities teacher preparation programs might provide to support this development across larger numbers of novices and contexts.

Calls for more ambitious teaching and skepticism toward university-based teacher preparation have given urgency to these questions and have been accompanied by calls for more robust evidence about how to prepare large numbers of effective teachers. In response, several studies have begun to examine the relationship between readily measurable aspects of teacher preparation programs—duration of clinical experiences, number of methods courses, the presence of a summative "capstone"—and K–12 student outcomes.[18] Some studies link the effectiveness of teacher candidates once they enter the workforce to clinical aspects of their teacher preparation. These include the level of teacher collaboration in the schools in which candidates are placed, the effectiveness of cooperating teachers' mentoring and instruction, and the match between the student demographics of candidates' clinical placements and those of the schools in which they take teaching positions.[19]

As alternative routes have expanded, a growing number of studies have also examined the relationship between different types of teacher preparation programs and K–12 student outcomes. Though these studies have reached mixed conclusions about whether university-based or alternate route preparation programs have a meaningfully distinct influence on teacher effectiveness, nearly all demonstrate substantially more variation in teacher effectiveness within programs than between them.[20] Few studies, however, have investigated associations between more specific, less easily assessable learning-to-teach opportunities offered in teacher education programs and beginning teachers' enactment of instruction aligned with ambitious learning standards. Further, few of these studies have examined associations between individual novice teachers' characteristics, teacher preparation learning opportunities, school resources, and their teaching practices.

Beginning teachers forge their instructional practice as they move between teacher preparation programs and K–12 schools. In addition, novices' own experiences as students, what Daniel Lortie termed the apprenticeship of observation,[21] shape their beliefs about teaching and learning. Research such as our DAI study, which includes multiple types of data collected directly from a large number of novice teachers across multiple program and school contexts and over time, is essential to understanding interactions among individual beginning teachers' characteristics, teacher preparation learning opportunities, school resources, and their association with novice teachers' development of ambitious teaching practices.

THE DEVELOPMENT OF AMBITIOUS INSTRUCTION STUDY

We designed the DAI study to address critical gaps in the current teacher education knowledge base that we identify above. The DAI study followed 175 elementary teacher candidates enrolled in five university-based teacher preparation programs as they transitioned from student teaching into their first two to three years of full-time teaching. Using a mixed-methods approach, we collected classroom observation, survey, and interview data from the beginning teachers between 2015 and 2019. This included surveys we collected about their learning opportunities in university courses and school-based field placements as well as their beliefs about and confidence in their abilities to teach mathematics and ELA. We then followed the teachers into their first two years of teaching, observing each teach three mathematics lessons and three ELA lessons each year. We also surveyed and interviewed the beginning teachers to understand their planning and instructional decisions, the resources they used, and their experiences with students, school-based teacher colleagues, principals, and others in their school contexts. We continued to observe thirty of these teachers during their third year of teaching, again observing three mathematics and three ELA lessons each, as well as collecting survey and interview data. Among these thirty teachers, we collected in-depth case study data from sixteen of them; this involved interviewing and observing each six times during their third year of teaching.

At the five participating universities, we interviewed teacher education program directors, field placement coordinators, and mathematics and ELA methods instructors and surveyed cooperating teachers and university supervisors who worked with the elementary candidates during their student teaching. After the beginning teachers started teaching full-time in schools, we surveyed their instructional coaches, mentor teachers, and principals. Throughout this book and in the methodological appendix, we provide more information on the different data sources and the strategies we used to analyze them.

PLATO AS A MEASURE OF AMBITIOUS INSTRUCTION

In total, we observed approximately one thousand mathematics and ELA lessons taught by the beginning teachers who participated in the DAI study. To analyze the ambitiousness of the novice teachers' mathematics and ELA instruction, we used the Protocol for Language

Arts Teaching Observation (PLATO).[22] PLATO assesses the quality of instructional practices in four domains: instructional scaffolding, disciplinary demand, representations and use of content, and classroom environment. We describe the protocol and these domains more fully in chapters 3 and 4.

PLATO has been used reliably in several studies to assess the relationship between instruction and student achievement gains. Many practices measured by PLATO predict teacher value-added measures.[23] Though Pamela Grossman and her colleagues originally developed PLATO to measure secondary ELA instruction, Julie Cohen modified PLATO to score mathematics lessons from the Measures of Effective Teaching (MET) study.[24] Further, the primary aspects of instruction measured by PLATO (i.e., disciplinary demand, instructional scaffolding, and representations and use of content) have been a focus of recent mathematics education reform efforts in the United States that seek to deepen students' engagement with and understanding of mathematics.[25] PLATO thus represents a practical, policy-relevant measure of instructional quality in mathematics and ELA.

THE BEGINNING TEACHERS

We followed a total of 175 beginning elementary teachers from their teacher preparation into their first two years of teaching between 2016 and 2019. This included eighty-three who completed a teaching survey as student teachers and who participated in classroom observations, surveys, and interviews as first-year teachers. Of these, sixty-four continued to participate in the same ways as second-year teachers and thirty continued to participate in the same ways as third-year teachers. In addition, another ninety-two novice teachers participated in surveys as student teachers and in their first and second years of teaching, but not through classroom observations. Data indicate that the 175 beginning teachers were similar to the other candidates at these universities, suggesting that the findings reported here are generalizable to the total sample of elementary candidates at the five universities.

Table 1.1 provides an overview of the teachers in our analytic sample. In terms of the full sample of 175 beginning teachers who participated in surveys for the DAI study, the sample was predominately female (94 percent), and white (88 percent). Only 6 percent of our sample identified as male, 8 percent as Black or African American, 2 percent as Asian, and 2 percent as Latino. The beginning teachers in our study took full-time teaching positions in ten different states and sixty-six different districts. In 2017–2018, roughly 89 percent of US public school elementary teachers were female and 78 percent identified as white. While largely comparable to the nation's teaching force, our sample included proportionally more white teachers.[26]

TABLE 1.1 Characteristics of the full sample of 175 beginning teacher participants

Teacher characteristics	
Female	0.94
White	0.88
Black or African American	0.08
Asian	0.02
Latino/a	0.02

Note: Teacher characteristics are based on the DAI Elementary Teacher Candidate survey.

THE TEACHER EDUCATION PROGRAMS

The five elementary teacher education programs in our sample—Cardinal University, Goldfinch University, Meadowlark University, Oriole University, and Robin University (all pseudonyms)—are public universities that collectively prepared approximately 450 to 500 elementary teacher candidates each year in 2015–2016 and 2016–2017 (the years when we collected data from elementary candidates in these programs). We selected these programs because each incorporated (a) research-based practices and/or (b) practice-based approaches in elementary mathematics and ELA methods courses and carefully structured student teaching to support candidates' development and enactment of ambitious instruction in mathematics and ELA. The five programs also varied in several ways, including characteristics of the universities (e.g., focus, location, and size) and the programs (e.g., length of student teaching and structure and sequence of methods courses and field experiences). This allowed us to examine variation in how opportunities to learn were structured and how this variation was associated with beginning teachers' instructional practice and other outcomes. Next, we provide brief descriptions of the elementary preparation programs at each university between 2015–2016 and 2016–2017. Table 1.2 includes descriptive information about program features.

Cardinal University

Cardinal University is a very highly active research institution located in a northeastern state. During 2015–2016 and 2016–2017, Cardinal offered one five-year elementary teacher education pathway and prepared approximately forty elementary teachers each year. Students took content courses throughout their four undergraduate years, completing eight courses (twenty-four credits) in one of four subject area majors (i.e., English, mathematics, science, or geography/history) and five courses distributed across the other subjects. They entered the preparation program their third year of undergraduate studies after successfully completing an admissions process that included an application and interview. Once admitted, students took education courses during their third and fourth years as undergraduates and during a fifth year as master's students. Candidates were in practicum placements for at least one day per week each semester during their first three semesters

TABLE 1.2 Descriptive information for the five elementary teacher preparation programs in the DAI study

Program features	*Cardinal University*	*Goldfinch University*	*Meadowlark University*	*Robin University*	*Oriole University*
Length of program	5-year BS/MA program	4-year BA program	5-year BA program plus MA credits	4-year BA program	5-year BS/MA program
Annual number of elementary graduates	40	100	150	150	60
Required course sequence	Yes	No	Yes	Yes	No
Cohort	Yes	Yes	Partial	Yes	No
Required math methods courses	1 math methods	2 math methods	2 math methods	2 math methods	1 math methods
Required ELA methods courses	2 ELA methods	2 ELA methods	2 ELA methods	3 ELA methods	3 ELA methods
Pre-student teaching field experience	6 hours/ week for 3 semesters	1 day/ week for 2 semesters	4 hours/ week for 2 semesters	6 hours/ week for 1 semester	1 day/ week for 1 semester
Length of student teaching	12 weeks	15 weeks	30 weeks	15 weeks	15 weeks
Length of lead responsibility for teaching	5 weeks	8 weeks	10 weeks	8 weeks	8 weeks
Timing of student teaching	Spring of 4th year	Fall or spring of 4th year	Fall and spring of 5th year	Spring of 4th year	Fall of 5th year

of the program, including the fall semester of their senior year. That fall they began working with the students and cooperating teachers with whom they would continue to work as they completed full-time student teaching for twelve weeks during spring semester. Candidates assumed lead responsibility for instruction for at least five of the twelve student teaching weeks. Students completed a practicum during their fifth year, which involved eighteen hours per week in clinical placements in both fall and spring semesters.

Elementary teacher candidates at Cardinal completed two ELA methods courses and one methods course in mathematics, science, and social studies, as well as courses in classroom management, child development, special education, assessment, and multicultural education. They were also required to complete a course taught in the university's mathematics department that was designed specifically for elementary teacher candidates. During student teaching, each teacher candidate was visited and observed by a university supervisor at least four times. In addition, the candidates met with their supervisors for midterm and final evaluative conferences. During their fifth year in the program, candidates took courses in content pedagogy, teacher leadership, and teaching diverse learners as well as seminars that supported their completion of a teacher-research inquiry related to their practicum. The elementary teacher education program at Cardinal featured a cohort model; students entered the program as juniors and proceeded as a cohort throughout the three-year program.

Goldfinch University

Goldfinch University is a teaching/community engagement institution located in a northeastern state. During 2015–2016 and 2016–2017, Goldfinch offered one elementary teacher education pathway and a four-year undergraduate bachelor's degree. During each of those years, the university prepared approximately one hundred elementary teachers. Students took content courses in a major designed for elementary education during their first two undergraduate years, completing between thirty-three and thirty-nine credits in one of six subject area majors (i.e., English, mathematics, general science/biology, general science/earth science, geography, or history), five courses distributed across general education requirements, and two educational foundations courses. They entered the preparation program their third year of undergraduate studies upon admission. Once admitted, students took elementary methods courses during their third and fourth years as undergraduates. Candidates were in practicum placements one day per week during the fall and spring semesters of their junior year and then completed full-time student teaching assignments for fifteen weeks during fall or spring semester of their senior year.

Elementary teacher candidates at Goldfinch completed two ELA methods courses, two mathematics methods courses, one science and one social studies methods course, as well as courses in general methods, educational technology, classroom management, child development, special education, and leadership. During student teaching, each teacher candidate was visited and observed by a university supervisor at least four times. The elementary teacher education program at Goldfinch included a cohort model; students entered the program their third year of undergraduate studies and proceeded as a cohort throughout the two-year program.

Meadowlark University

Meadowlark University is a very highly active research institution located in a Midwestern state. During 2015–2016 and 2016–2017, Meadowlark offered one elementary teacher education pathway, an undergraduate bachelor's degree with a fifth year of master's course credits, and prepared approximately 150 elementary teachers each year. Students took their content and methods courses during their fourth year as undergraduates and in their fifth year (i.e., for master's credits). All candidates completed two semester-long practicum placements in their fourth year and a thirty-week student teaching placement in their fifth year. They were required to assume lead responsibility for instruction for ten of the thirty weeks.

Elementary teacher candidates at Meadowlark were required to complete two ELA methods courses and two mathematics methods courses.

They also took courses in social studies methods, science methods, classroom management, child development, special education, and multicultural education. During student teaching, each teacher candidate was visited and observed by a university supervisor approximately six times. In addition, they met with their supervisor for midterm and final evaluative conferences. The elementary teacher education program at Meadowlark featured a cohort model; students entered the program as juniors and proceeded as a cohort throughout the three-year program.

Oriole University

Oriole University is a very highly active research institution located in a mid-Atlantic state. During 2015–2016 and 2016–2017, Oriole offered two elementary teacher education pathways: Path A, a joint undergraduate bachelor's/master of teaching degree, and Path B, a two-year postgraduate master of teaching degree. Oriole prepared approximately sixty elementary teachers each year in 2015–2016 and 2016–2017. Students in Path A took the majority of their education coursework during their fourth year as undergraduates and completed student teaching in their fifth year (as master's degree students). Students in Path B completed their content and methods courses during their first year in the program and completed student teaching in their second year. All candidates completed two semester-long practicum placements. Their student teaching placements lasted approximately fifteen weeks. The candidates assumed lead responsibility for instruction for eight of the fifteen weeks.

Elementary teacher candidates at Oriole were required to complete three ELA methods courses, one mathematics methods course, one social studies methods course, and one science methods course. They also took one course in each of the following: general principles of curriculum, instruction, and assessment; classroom management; child development; and special education. During student teaching, elementary candidates submitted videos of six lessons and lesson plans; their university supervisors interacted with them through video conferences and provided feedback through a digital platform. The elementary teacher education program at Oriole did not feature a cohort model.

Robin University

Robin University is a highly active research institution located in a mid-Atlantic state. During 2015–2016 and 2016–2017, Robin offered one elementary teacher education pathway, a joint undergraduate bachelor of arts/master of teaching degree, and prepared approximately 150 elementary teachers each year. Students took their content and methods courses during their fourth year as undergraduates and their fifth year as master's students. All candidates completed a practicum experience and a fifteen-week student teaching placement in their fifth year; they were required to assume lead responsibility for instruction for eight of the fifteen weeks.

Elementary teacher candidates at Robin were required to complete three ELA methods courses, two mathematics methods courses, one social studies methods course, and one science methods course. They also took a classroom management course, a child development course, a special education course, an assessment course, and a multicultural education course. During student teaching, each teacher candidate was visited and observed by a university supervisor approximately four times. The elementary teacher education program at Robin featured a cohort model; students entered the program as juniors and proceeded as a cohort throughout the three-year program.

OVERVIEW OF BOOK

In the subsequent chapters, we draw on our analyses of data we collected as part of the DAI study to develop insights that teacher preparation and school induction programs can use to support beginning teachers' development of ambitious instruction. Chapter 2 describes elementary teacher candidates' opportunities to learn, try out, and receive feedback on (a) general teaching strategies, (b) ambitious teaching strategies in mathematics and ELA, and (c) strategies for teaching diverse learners in teacher preparation courses and field placements at the five universities in the DAI study. We describe differences in learning opportunities within and across programs as well as variation in candidates' perceptions of the degree to which their programs were coherent. In particular, there was notable variation within, but not between, programs with regard to opportunities to learn general teaching strategies and strategies for teaching diverse learners. In addition, variation was evident in candidates' reported opportunities to examine representations of ambitious teaching strategies in mathematics and ELA and to try out the strategies with peers in methods courses. This chapter also draws on interview data to provide examples and illustrations of these findings.

In chapter 3, we draw primarily on quantitative analyses to report on beginning teachers' enactment of ambitious instructional practices in mathematics and ELA and the factors, including teacher preparation learning opportunities, that were associated with such enactment. In the first section of this chapter, we document average PLATO scores in both mathematics and ELA for the first- and second-year teachers in our sample and identify the domains of ambitious practices in which novices developed their skills between their first and second years. The second section reports on significant associations between candidates' learning opportunities in teacher preparation courses and field placements and their implementation of ambitious instruction as first-year teachers in mathematics and ELA. In the final section, we describe significant associations between candidates' learning opportunities in courses and clinical placements and their implementation of ambitious ELA practices as second-year teachers.

Chapter 4 presents in-depth case studies of three elementary teachers drawn from the sample of thirty beginning teachers we followed from student teaching into their third year of teaching. The three teachers' mathematics and ELA instruction was among the more ambitious in the sample of thirty and the larger sample. Drawing on our analyses of observation and interview data, the chapter explores how the ways in which the novice teachers made sense of, selected, and adapted resources from teacher preparation and their school settings assisted them in developing and enacting ambitious instructional practices. Using the notion of personal sense drawn from sociocultural learning theory, the chapter highlights how the novice teachers' resource use both was shaped by and shaped their knowledge and beliefs about teaching and learning, their desire to establish themselves as competent professionals, and their emotional engagement in their work and with their students and colleagues.

Chapter 5 looks across the previous chapters and draws on quantitative and qualitative data across all four years of the DAI study to present major themes related to preparing novice teachers to teach mathematics and ELA ambitiously. We then present implications for practice regarding preservice courses and field placements as well as school-based supports for novice teachers. The methodological appendix, which will be of particular interest to researchers, describes in detail our teacher education program sample, our beginning teacher sample, our data collection strategies, and the ways in which we analyzed the classroom observation, survey, and interview data for the DAI study. It concludes by outlining next steps for future research on teacher preparation and novice teacher development.

CHAPTER 2

Opportunities to Learn How to Teach Ambitiously

Ambitious instruction aims to foster all students' robust understanding of disciplinary concepts and practices by engaging them in cognitively demanding tasks. It centers students' ideas and sensemaking, positioning students as capable learners and the funds of knowledge they bring with them from their families and communities as critical resources for their own and their classmates' learning. Rather than a set of routines, moves, or strategies to be employed generically, ambitious instruction represents a set of practices that teachers adapt in response to their particular students' interests, needs, and identities. As David Stroupe and colleagues assert, teaching ambitiously requires that beginning teachers cultivate their skills enacting particular practices *and* employing judgment, compassion, and knowledge as they plan, teach, and reflect on their instruction.[1]

Calls for beginning teachers to teach more ambitiously have placed increased attention on the types of learning opportunities that teacher preparation programs do—and should—provide teacher candidates. University-based teacher preparation programs have long been criticized for emphasizing knowledge about teaching rather than preparing beginning teachers for the complexities of actual classroom teaching.[2] Some of these critiques come from beginning teachers themselves, who often view student teaching as the most valuable part of their preparation, while disparaging coursework as too theoretical.[3] Preparing beginning teachers who can teach ambitiously calls for better understanding how teacher preparation programs can provide novices opportunities to build their knowledge about ambitious instructional practices and their knowledge of how, when, and why to enact and modify these practices for and with their particular students. Teacher education programs must offer a range of *opportunities to learn* not only about important content and practices for teaching but also how to use what they learn.[4]

In this chapter, we explore the opportunities to learn which the five university-based teacher preparation programs that participated in our Development of Ambitious Instruction (DAI) study provided their teacher candidates. Our overview of the programs in chapter 1 detailed differences in the number of English language arts (ELA) and mathematics methods courses they required elementary candidates to complete and the timing and duration of student teaching placements. We chose to study these programs partly because of this variation. In this chapter, we examine the opportunities to learn that the programs provided their candidates within university courses and through field experiences. Identifying how teacher education programs can best equip beginning teachers requires us to better understand the learning opportunities the programs do and can provide novices at this more granular level. In addition to identifying these opportunities to learn, we explore issues related to program coherence. Teacher education scholars argue that the lack of a shared vision of quality teaching across courses and between courses and field placements limits the impact programs can have on novices' teaching by making it difficult for beginning teachers to develop a conceptual understanding of teaching and the practices to enact it.[5]

In the following sections, we first define opportunities to learn (OTL) and program coherence, attending to their relationship to ambitious instruction. We then describe the data sources we used to examine OTLs and coherence in relation to the five programs in the DAI study and present the findings of our analysis of these data. We draw our data primarily from our Elementary Teacher Candidate survey, which we administered to beginning teachers after they completed student teaching. We recognize that teacher candidates' opportunities to learn are influenced by the learners themselves, the nature of the tasks they engage with, and the pedagogical approaches that teacher educators employ.[6] While teacher preparation programs might intend to provide particular types of learning opportunities, how teacher candidates experience the opportunities depends on their own knowledge, beliefs, and goals.[7] Our focus on candidates' perceptions of teacher preparation opportunities to learn and on program coherence thus provides partial insight into both. At the same time, a focus on candidate perceptions is valuable given that it is ultimately the teacher candidates who must take up and put to use what they learn in their preparation programs as they become teachers of record.

DEFINING OPPORTUNITIES TO LEARN AND PROGRAM COHERENCE IN TEACHER PREPARATION

While teacher education researchers have conceptualized OTL in a variety of ways, much survey-based research uses William Schmidt and colleagues' (2011) definition of OTLs in teacher education as "the content to which future teachers are exposed to as part of their teacher preparation programs."[8] In their international studies of mathematics education, Schmidt and colleagues further highlight three types of content: *content knowledge* (i.e., knowledge of mathematics, knowledge of literature and/or composition, etc.), *pedagogical content knowledge* (i.e., knowledge of how students learn content and how to teach it), and *general pedagogical knowledge* (i.e., knowledge of how to motivate students, how to design learning tasks, how to organize small groups, etc.).[9] We examine exposure to this knowledge as part of university coursework and field experiences, especially student teaching. Earlier research documents the significance of candidates' self-reported opportunities to learn general and content-specific pedagogical strategies in both coursework and student teaching placements for beginning elementary teachers' effectiveness as measured by tests of student achievement.[10] Few of these studies, however, examine associations between these OTLs and beginning teachers' instruction.

A growing number of studies of practice-based teacher education have begun to identify the types of learning opportunities that can equip teacher candidates with the knowledge and skills to enact and continue to develop ambitious teaching practices as they transition into in-service teaching.[11] Practice-based teacher education focuses teacher candidates' learning on core teaching practices that support rigorous student learning, are teachable within a combination of university courses and clinical experiences, and are foundational for novice teachers' subsequent professional development.

Teacher educators have begun to develop teacher education pedagogies that can assist teacher candidates in building their skills in enacting core teaching practices. Pamela Grossman and her colleagues highlight the potential of three types of teacher education pedagogies for supporting beginning teachers' development of ambitious teaching practices–decomposition, representations, and approximations. *Decomposition* pedagogies deepen teacher candidates' understanding of ambitious instructional practices through examining the practices' component parts. *Representation* pedagogies engage candidates in analyzing representations of ambitious teaching through examining lesson plans, for example, or observing in-person or videotaped enactments of ambitious teaching. Finally, *approximation* pedagogies, including rehearsals and simulations, afford teacher candidates opportunities to enact core practices and receive feedback on their performance in increasingly complex contexts.[12] For instance, rehearsing facilitating a text-based discussion with peers and instructors in a university methods course and then with K–12 students in student teaching settings allows teacher candidates to build their skills in posing authentic questions and pressing students to justify and elaborate their interpretations with textual evidence and logical reasoning.

Taken together, decomposition, representation, and approximation pedagogies represent a set of OTLs that can assist beginning teachers in building their knowledge about and skills enacting ambitious instruction as they transition from preservice to in-service teaching.[13] To date, most studies of these pedagogies include small numbers of beginning teachers typically from a single teacher preparation program and in a single subject area. This limits our insights into how larger numbers of beginning teachers across multiple programs experience these OTLs and how the pedagogies contribute to novices' efforts to enact ambitious instruction across multiple contexts and subject areas.

Several teacher education scholars interested in practice-based teacher education are exploring how providing teacher candidates opportunities to build their knowledge and fluency enacting ambitious instructional practices can support more equitable learning outcomes for students who have been historically marginalized because of their race, gender, language, and socioeconomic status. Jessica Thompson and her colleagues, for example, bring a critical equity perspective to their work in science teacher education to assist beginning teachers in developing culturally and linguistically sustaining ambitious instructional practices that center students' cultures, identities, and funds of knowledge.[14] Similarly, Angela Calabrese Barton and her colleagues, also in science education, call for grounding a focus on ambitious practices in a larger vision of justice-oriented teaching that expands opportunities for students to engage with core disciplinary concepts and practices in culturally relevant ways and disrupts racialized, gendered, and classed systems of power that operate in routine teaching practices. As Calabrese Barton and colleagues argue, integrating concerns for equity and justice into conceptions of ambitious instruction "foregrounds the political and humanizing dimensions of teaching/learning, which values students as whole people, whose knowledge/wisdom, experiences and fraught histories are integral to disciplinary engagement."[15]

Such efforts have begun to identify the opportunities to learn that beginning teachers will need to enact ambitious instructional practices in ways that promote more equitable student learning outcomes. These include opportunities for beginning teachers to interrogate their own and others' identities as part of developing a critical understanding of how systems of power operate and can be disrupted in everyday classroom teaching and learning practices; to learn about and prioritize students' communities, cultures, and funds of knowledge; to design classrooms and tasks that support each student's full participation; and to challenge disciplinary norms and practices that reinscribe inequities and injustice.[16]

Program coherence

A growing body of scholarship has argued for the importance of teacher education program coherence.[17] This work highlights the importance of conceptual and structural coherence. *Conceptual coherence* refers to the extent to which preparation programs convey a shared vision of teaching and learning within and across courses, as well as between courses and student teaching experiences. For example, this might include literacy, mathematics, science, and history/social studies methods courses for candidates in the same program that all focus on elementary teaching practices that promote students' conceptual understanding of disciplinary content. Alternatively, a program might emphasize teaching in specific contexts or working toward social justice across the range of its courses. When examining conceptual coherence, it is important to consider whether a program articulates teaching strategies or approaches that embody its vision. Emphases on particular strategies for teaching elementary students or particular content (e.g., focus on diverse learners) may offer insight into ways that the program enacts its vision with teacher candidates.[18]

Another way teacher preparation programs can convey coherence to teacher candidates is through *structural coherence*. Structural coherence is supported when instructional approaches highlighted in methods courses are reinforced by those used by cooperating teachers in field placements. This might include, for instance, emphasizing similar approaches to classroom management in courses, field experiences, and assessments of candidates during student teaching. In contrast, a program might exhibit weaker structural coherence if the kinds of instructional practices emphasized in courses do not align with those enacted by cooperating teachers in student teaching placements.

We posit that program coherence is important in preparing beginning teachers to teach ambitiously because it supports their conceptual understanding of teaching. The visions of teaching and learning that novice teachers appropriate through teacher preparation shape the teacher identities they construct and the types of teachers they aspire to be and eventually become in their early careers and beyond. Programs that offer clear visions of teaching and learning that are reinforced across preparation experiences can provide novice teachers with frames or sets of principles with which to make sense of, critique, adapt, and/or reject teaching practices that they read about and observe in their teacher preparation programs and that they themselves experienced as students.

We recognize that these two constructs—opportunities to learn to teach and program coherence—are distinct. Teacher candidates can make sense of the types and quality of the OTLs their programs offer separate from their perceptions of whether their programs provide a coherent vision of teaching and learning. At the same time, as Sharon

Feiman-Nemser and colleagues argue, candidates' perception of how well the OTLs and the messages about teaching and learning that their programs offer are aligned matter.[19] As Feiman-Nemser and colleagues note, however, too often beginning teachers can become disillusioned when teacher preparation programs offer them opportunities and resources to develop visions of ambitious teaching without also providing them opportunities to try out and cultivate their skills enacting such visions.[20] This contributes to novice teachers employing ambitious instructional practices partially or eschewing them altogether as they adopt practices that limit their students' learning and might perpetuate rather than disrupt inequities.

Data sources

In this chapter, we draw primarily on data from the Elementary Teacher Candidate survey we created and administered to beginning teachers participating in our DAI study when they were completing student teaching placements or soon after. For all teacher candidates except those enrolled at Cardinal University, student teaching occurred in the final semester and/or final school year of their preparation program. Administering the survey at this time allowed us to capture candidates' perceptions of the learning opportunities they had experienced across their program. In total, we drew on survey data from five hundred elementary teacher candidates across the five universities in three states who participated in the DAI study during their final year of teacher preparation. We included two cohorts of candidates in our study: one cohort was in their final year of preparation in 2015–2016, and the other was in their final year in 2016–2017. In reporting our findings, we grouped the cohorts at each institution together.

The Elementary Teacher Candidate survey included several items that asked teacher candidates to report on their opportunities to learn about general teaching methods, ambitious instructional practices in ELA and mathematics, and instructional strategies for teaching diverse students. For example, we asked them about opportunities to examine representations of the practices in video or written cases and opportunities to try them out with peers in methods courses. In addition, the survey asked them about opportunities during clinical placements to learn, try out, and receive feedback on their attempts to enact the practices.

In addition to survey items about OTLs, we also draw here on survey items that explored elementary candidates' perceptions of program coherence. In terms of program coherence, survey questions asked about the extent to which candidates agreed about the following: that their program articulates a clear vision of teaching and learning; that they hear similar views about teaching and learning across courses; that what they learn in methods courses reflects what they observe in their field experiences or their student teaching classroom; that they have gotten to know the other students in their program well; that they feel part of a larger group of people who all share common values with respect to teaching; and that the criteria by which they are evaluated as a student teacher are consistent with what they are taught in their methods courses.

We also draw on interview data that we collected from teacher education program directors, field placement coordinators, and ELA and mathematics methods instructors. In 2015–2016 and 2016–2017, at each of the five universities, we interviewed the director of teacher education, the field placement coordinator, and ELA and mathematics methods instructors. In addition, we interviewed first- and second-year teachers who graduated from each of the five universities in 2015–2016 and 2016–2017 and continued participating in our study during their first few years of full-time teaching.

Analytic strategy

We used several statistical techniques, including descriptive statistics, one-way analyses of variance (ANOVAs), and paired sample *t*-tests, to examine differences in OTLs and program coherence between university programs. We relied on a series of simple descriptive statistics, including means and standard deviations, to report on patterns in candidates' OTLs and perceptions of program coherence by cohort and by university. We conducted one-way ANOVAs with Bonferroni tests to identify statistically significant differences between university programs' OTLs and program coherence. We also employed paired sample *t*-tests to identify statistically significant differences between university programs with regard to OTL in mathematics versus OTL in ELA. Finally, we selected interview data to include in this chapter in order to illustrate findings from these analyses of the survey data.

Please note that the sample sizes for each elementary teacher preparation program sometimes vary in the descriptive results we present below because of missing data (e.g., a given teacher candidate may have answered most of but not all the survey items). In addition, the sample sizes varied across programs, given that some programs were substantially larger than others (in the number of elementary teacher candidates they graduated each year).

OPPORTUNITIES TO LEARN WITHIN AND ACROSS PREPARATION PROGRAMS

In this section, we report on descriptive findings across the five preparation programs regarding elementary teacher candidates' opportunities to learn (a) general teaching strategies, (b) ambitious teaching strategies in mathematics and ELA, and (c) strategies for teaching diverse learners. In addition, we draw on interview data to provide examples and illustrations of the descriptive findings. With regard to (a), we found notable variation within, but not between, programs. In terms of (b), there was clear variation in candidates' reported opportunities to examine representations of the ambitious teaching strategies in mathematics and ELA and to try them out with peers in methods courses. Finally, in terms of (c), while most candidates across all five programs reported having opportunities to learn about strategies for teaching diverse learners, variation was evident within programs.

Opportunities to learn general teaching strategies

General teaching strategies include unit and lesson planning, principles and theories of instruction, ways to set up group work, ways to engage and motivate students, and formative and summative assessment.[21] Table 2.1 reports the mean responses of candidates from each preparation program to questions about the opportunities they had in their programs to learn about general principles and theories of instruction and general methods of teaching. As the table indicates, candidates across the programs had opportunities to discuss and/or enact general teaching principles and theories and methods. Mean responses to the survey items ranged on a four-point scale from 3.25 among Goldfinch candidates to 3.45 among Cardinal and Oriole candidates. We did not find statistically different responses between programs in candidates' reported opportunities to learn such strategies.

We did find notable variation in candidates' responses within programs. The standard deviations for these two survey items ranged from .533 to .769; this means that within the same preparation program,

TABLE 2.1 Teacher candidates' opportunities to learn general teaching strategies across the five elementary teacher education programs in the DAI study

	Cardinal	*Goldfinch*	*Meadowlark*	*Oriole*	*Robin*
General principles and theories of instruction	3.450 (.769)	3.250 (.683)	3.308 (.729)	3.452 (.621)	3.339 (.621)
General methods of teaching (includes lesson planning; motivating students)	3.667 (.572)	3.375 (.619)	3.610 (.626)	3.663 (.533)	3.752 (.533)
Number of participants	60	16	159	104	165

Note: Scale: 1 = none; 2 = touched on it briefly; 3 = spent time discussing or doing it; 4 = had extensive opportunity.

candidates' reports of OTLs in general principles and methods of teaching differed from the mean response by roughly one-half to three-quarters of a point on a four-point scale. More specifically, some candidates reported touching briefly on general principles and methods of teaching, while others within the same program reported having extensive opportunities to discuss them.

As described by the Cardinal University director of teacher education, a seminar that elementary candidates took concurrent with their student teaching placement illustrates the types of opportunities the preparation programs provided candidates to learn about general teaching principles and methods: "This seminar is designed to help candidates analyze, reflect [on], and improve their teaching . . . how to establish routines, how to establish relationships with students. That's a big piece of it. Another piece we've put in place is the analysis of their impact on student learning. Candidates take one of the lesson sequences that they're teaching, make a pre- and post-assessment, collect student work, and then analyze it."

As exemplified by this comment, the programs offered candidates opportunities to learn about general teaching methods such as establishing classroom routines and building relationships with students. In addition, candidates learned about and engaged in lesson planning and assessment, as they were required to plan and teach a sequence of lessons that included designing and administering assessments. They also analyzed student work and performance on these assessments to consider how their teaching supported their students' learning.

Opportunities to learn ambitious teaching strategies in mathematics and English language arts

Given our focus on ambitious instruction in both subjects, our Elementary Teacher Candidate survey asked candidates about their opportunities to learn about, try out, and receive feedback on twelve practices associated with ambitious instruction. In both subjects, these practices included designing high cognitive demand tasks, teaching strategies for learning content, connecting content to students' prior content knowledge, connecting content to students' personal/cultural experiences, facilitating students' use of technology in doing mathematics or in reading and writing, facilitating classroom discussions, managing time and student behavior during instruction, and providing students feedback in learning content. In mathematics, the practices also included (a) using representations to develop students' mathematics understanding and (b) identifying and responding to common patterns of student thinking in mathematics (e.g., strategies, misconceptions). In ELA, the practices also included (a) using analogies and/or examples to develop students' understanding of ELA concepts and (b) identifying and responding to students' interpretations of ELA texts.[22] Drawing on literature on practice-based teacher education pedagogies, we asked candidates if they had opportunities to examine these practices in video or written cases and try them with peers in methods course. We also asked if they had opportunities during student teaching to try them out with elementary students and receive feedback on them. Table 2.2 reports on candidates' responses.

To calculate the mean responses for each preparation program for a given response category (e.g., examined in video or written case), we added up the number of times each candidate responded yes for each of the twelve ambitious teaching strategies and assigned them a percentage (e.g., if they responded yes six out of twelve times, they received .50). The mean for a given program represents the average percentage across all the candidates in that program for that response category. For example, the .396 for Cardinal for "examined in video or written case" means that Cardinal candidates responded yes on average for almost 40 percent, or close to five of the twelve mathematics teaching strategies.

As Table 2.2 shows, elementary teacher candidates in all five programs reported having the opportunity to use ambitious strategies in mathematics and ELA with elementary students during student

TABLE 2.2 Teacher candidates' opportunities to learn ambitious teaching strategies in mathematics and ELA across the five elementary teacher education programs in the DAI study

	Cardinal	*Goldfinch*	*Meadowlark*	*Oriole*	*Robin*
Mathematics: examined in video or written case	0.396 (.394)	0.206 (.329)	0.582 (.372)	0.529 (.349)	0.494 (.381)
Mathematics: tried with peers in methods course	0.719 (.299)	0.388 (.356)	0.642 (.327)	0.568 (.283)	0.690 (.305)
Mathematics: tried with elementary students in student teaching	0.888 (.176)	0.900 (.131)	0.916 (.186)	0.792 (.255)	0.860 (.181)
Mathematics: received feedback	0.660 (.339)	0.467 (.436)	0.639 (.380)	0.493 (.341)	0.622 (.333)
Mathematics: Number of Participants	60	15	156	97	162
ELA: examined in video or written case	0.290 (.379)	0.156 (.294)	0.506 (.382)	0.452 (.408)	0.316 (.382)
ELA: tried with peers in methods course	0.523 (.377)	0.413 (.396)	0.570 (.374)	0.539 (.373)	0.457 (.401)
ELA: tried with elementary students in student teaching	0.900 (.197)	0.906 (.153)	0.898 (.230)	0.805 (.293)	0.795 (.300)
ELA: received feedback	0.615 (.409)	0.500 (.460)	0.610 (.408)	0.484 (.364)	0.468 (.401)
ELA: Number of participants	60	16	156	98	164

teaching. In both mathematics and ELA, candidates reported that during student teaching, they had the opportunities to try out roughly 80–90 percent of strategies, or ten or eleven of the twelve teaching practices. Across the preparation programs, there was more variation in candidates' reported opportunities to examine representations of the ambitious teaching strategies and to try them out with peers in methods courses. In mathematics, Goldfinch candidates reported having opportunities to examine representations of roughly 20 percent, or two of the ambitious teaching strategies, while candidates in Meadowlark reported having opportunities to examine representations of close to 60 percent, or seven of the twelve practices.

Similarly, in ELA, candidates in Goldfinch reported examining representations of roughly 16 percent, or two of the ambitious teaching strategies, while candidates in Meadowlark reported examining representations of 50 percent, or six of the twelve strategies. Further, while candidates across the five programs reported trying out between 40 percent and nearly 60 percent, or roughly five to seven, of the ambitious ELA teaching strategies with peers in their method courses, in mathematics their opportunities ranged from Goldfinch candidates trying out roughly 40 percent, or five practices, to Cardinal candidates trying out 70 percent, or eight practices, with peers in methods courses.

Overall, the five programs provided candidates a range of opportunities to learn about and try out ambitious teaching practices in mathematics and ELA. At Cardinal, where candidates reported having opportunities to try from half to most of the ambitious practices in ELA and mathematics, respectively, with peers in their methods courses, faculty had a long history of engaging candidates in microteaching. At Meadowlark and Oriole, methods faculty employed practice-based teacher education pedagogies that, for example, engaged candidates in rehearsing multimodal literacy lessons and facilitating learning centers with their peers or selecting and using manipulatives to build students' mathematical understanding and skill with their methods instructor who acted as an elementary student.

Finally, we note that the standard deviations for most of the survey items related to ambitious teaching strategies were relatively low (i.e., in most cases, they were below .40, or less than one-half point on a four-point scale). This indicates that candidates within the five programs generally had similar perceptions of the OTLs related to ambitious teaching practices. This differs from the within-program variation we find in relation to candidates' reports on their opportunities to learn general teaching methods and, as we show in the next section, strategies for teaching diverse learners.

Opportunities to learn strategies for teaching diverse learners

Strategies for teaching diverse learners include maintaining students' cultural competency and cultural integrity, providing equitable opportunities for participation, and maintaining high expectations for and promoting student achievement among all students.[23] Research indicates that opportunities to learn about strategies for teaching diverse students during preservice preparation are associated with elementary teacher candidates' beliefs and self-efficacy related to working with diverse learners.[24] Table 2.3 indicates that most candidates across all

TABLE 2.3 Teacher candidates' opportunities to learn about strategies for teaching diverse learners across the five elementary teacher education programs in the DAI study

	Cardinal	*Goldfinch*	*Meadowlark*	*Oriole*	*Robin*
Instruction for racially/ethnically diverse students	3.150 (.840)	3.188 (.834)	3.484 (.674)	3.048 (.702)	3.303 (.702)
Instruction for linguistically diverse students	3.233 (.831)	3.125 (.619)	3.340 (.673)	2.952 (.716)	2.982 (.745)
Instruction for socioeconomically diverse students	3.017 (.930)	3.250 (.683)	3.352 (.772)	2.769 (.740)	3.109 (.749)
Gain knowledge about the communities of the students you are likely to teach	2.983 (.833)	3.000 (.730)	3.289 (.749)	2.769 (.815)	3.048 (.825)
Develop specific strategies for teaching English language learners (those with limited English proficiency)	3.417 (.696)	3.000 (.730)	2.987 (.842)	2.885 (.728)	2.673 (.912)
Consider the relationship between education and equity	2.717 (.958)	3.000 (.816)	3.094 (.877)	2.952 (.781)	2.800 (.828)
Number of participants	60	16	159	104	165

Note: Scale: 1 = none; 2 = touched on it briefly; 3 = spent time discussing or doing it; 4 = had extensive opportunity.

five programs reported having opportunities to learn about strategies for teaching diverse learners. In particular, most candidates at all five programs reported either spending time discussing or engaging in strategies for teaching diverse students or having extensive opportunity to learn about the strategies.

Again, however, we note the considerable variation in candidates' responses within preparation programs. The standard deviations for these items ranged from .619 to .930, or over one-half of a point to nearly one point on a four-point scale. This indicates that within the same program some candidates reported touching briefly on one or more strategies for teaching diverse learners while other candidates reported having extensive opportunities to discuss them.

In addition, candidates at Meadowlark reported having more opportunities to learn strategies for teaching diverse learners than did candidates at Oriole or Robin (at the level of $p < .05$). Meadowlark focused on preparing teacher candidates to teach diverse students throughout its elementary teacher education program. Before admission to the program, all Meadowlark students took a course focused on issues related to equity, diversity, social structures, and power. This course was designed to help candidates interrogate their beliefs about teaching children from diverse backgrounds and to disrupt deficit views of these children and their communities. Meadowlark faculty further integrated attention to working with diverse groups of students into its content-specific methods courses, as the director of teacher education noted:

> We don't have a course called teaching with technology, or teaching students with special needs, or any of those kinds of courses that you find in other programs. [Instead], we try to integrate those ideas into the content area methods courses. In the math methods course, there should be integrated focus on how do you teach math using technology? How do you teach math to students with special needs? How do you teach math to English learners? All of those ideas that might be in a general course are in the content methods courses here. That's one distinctive characteristic of our program.

Meadowlark methods instructors echoed this focus on integrating throughout the program opportunities for candidates to learn to teach diverse groups of students. For example, a mathematics methods instructor explained that Meadowlark's sequence of two mathematics methods courses engaged candidates "deeply" with ideas related to "meeting the needs of diverse learners and getting to know your students," including considering multiple ways to allow students to exhibit their competence. This instructor went on to explain that a shared goal of the Meadowlark mathematics methods coursework was to help candidates "start to think of mathematical practices of (the) community and funds of knowledge in the community that we can build on in the classroom." These asset-focused perspectives permeated instructors' descriptions of content-specific coursework. Instructors viewed these perspectives as providing a foundation for Meadowlark candidates' development of ambitious mathematical instructional practices that supported equitable student outcomes.

PROGRAM COHERENCE WITHIN AND ACROSS PROGRAMS

Conceptual coherence is evident when elementary teacher candidates perceive a shared vision of teaching and learning across their different courses and between their coursework and clinical placements. Structural coherence is evident when cooperating teachers in clinical placements employ teaching, assessment, and classroom management practices that are similar to or aligned with those promoted in methods courses. Preparation programs that feature high levels of program coherence are likely to prepare beginning teachers who can employ rigorous, high-quality instructional practices.[25]

Candidates at all five programs participating in the DAI study agreed or strongly agreed that their programs were coherent. This included agreeing or strongly agreeing that their program articulated a clear vision of teaching and learning, that what they learned in methods courses reflected what they observed in their field experiences, and that the criteria used to evaluate their performance during student teaching were consistent with the knowledge, skills, and practices they encountered in their methods courses. See Table 2.4.

TABLE 2.4 Teacher candidates' perceptions of teacher preparation program coherence across the five elementary teacher education programs in the DAI study

	Cardinal	*Goldfinch*	*Meadowlark*	*Oriole*	*Robin*
My program articulates a clear vision of teaching and learning	3.600 (.527)	3.188 (.911)	3.509 (.635)	3.413 (.533)	3.527 (.525)
I hear similar views about teaching and learning across courses	3.450 (.594)	3.188 (.834)	3.440 (.569)	3.327 (.548)	3.424 (.596)
What I learn in methods courses reflects what I observe in my field experiences or in my own classroom	3.417 (.619)	3.125 (.719)	3.145 (.745)	3.125 (.586)	3.255 (.687)
I have gotten to know the other students in my program well	3.500 (.624)	3.688 (.479)	3.484 (.664)	3.183 (.679)	3.576 (.596)
I feel part of a larger group of people who all share common values with respect to teaching	3.433 (.745)	3.625 (.500)	3.547 (.643)	3.288 (.634)	3.594 (.583)
The criteria by which I am evaluated as a student teacher/intern are consistent with what I am taught in my methods courses	3.317 (.770)	3.125 (.806)	3.296 (.699)	3.279 (.615)	3.467 (.547)
Number of participants	60	16	159	104	165

Note: Scale: 1 = strongly disagree; 2 = disagree; 3 = agree; 4 = strongly agree.

For example, the Cardinal elementary preparation program highlighted robust clinical partnerships with the K–12 school districts where candidates engaged in field experiences. Cardinal candidates completed elementary school classroom placements every semester of the program and enrolled in clinical seminar courses concurrent with them. During the fall semester of their senior year, Cardinal elementary candidates completed subject-specific methods courses in mathematics, ELA, science, and social studies while also working with students and a cooperating teacher in an elementary school classroom for four to six hours. They completed full-time student teaching in the same classroom during the spring semester. As the Cardinal director explained, candidates were "learning methods and then they're trying them out in their placements." In addition, the Cardinal program director noted that university-based clinical faculty maintained "constant communication" with administrators and lead teachers in partnering districts to identify and maintain "quality" cooperating teachers and placements. The university-school partnerships thus contributed to conceptual and structural coherence in the Cardinal elementary preparation program.

A first-year teacher who graduated from Cardinal described how this program coherence helped her develop her ELA teaching, especially with emergent bilingual and multilingual students. Cardinal faculty worked together to integrate a focus on teaching strategies for emergent bilingual and multilingual learners across the elementary methods courses. The Cardinal graduate felt that "the most helpful" content she learned during teacher preparation was "the strategies of working with EL [English learners] students, especially because we talked a lot about them." She noted that during student teaching, these strategies "were really important for me to pay attention to and that's what's really stuck with me." The first-year teacher's comment illustrates one way in which Cardinal candidates were exposed to similar views of teaching and learning across their courses and their field placements.

At Robin, the elementary teacher education program director and methods instructors consistently emphasized their efforts to promote coherence across courses and between courses and clinical placements. The Robin program director highlighted the program's "constructivist approach to teaching and learning" and described how the program deliberately hired faculty who shared this vision of teaching and learning. Faculty members at Robin also worked to ensure that they promoted similar teaching practices across their courses and candidates' field placements. One mathematics methods instructor noted: "We actually work with the science methods teachers. For example, SMART goals. We were trying to get [candidates] to understand SMART goals and we worked one on one with them in making the goals and how to implement them. That's done a lot in our courses. We actually work with those other professors to make sure that that's implemented and done across the methods sections." In short, the elementary teacher education faculty at Robin worked together to engage elementary candidates in developing a shared set of teaching strategies.

Two of the elementary ELA methods instructors at Robin also spoke about how they promoted coherence between courses and field experiences. One explained, "We have a lot of conversations about what [candidates] are seeing out in the schools and how that can connect to what I am talking about in class." The other ELA methods instructor added that she required candidates in her course to design, justify, and teach fluency minilessons during clinical placements. She noted that the assignment "forces them to . . . build that bridge and make that link between what they're seeing and what we're doing. And they do that every time they do a minilesson." As these explanations indicate, instructors at Robin shared a common focus on helping candidates make connections between their coursework and their field experiences.

In our interviews, Robin graduates described how they drew on what they learned in their preparation programs. For example, one graduate explained how she regularly thought about the concepts from her mathematics methods courses as she planned mathematics lessons: "So the CRA model is definitely what I'm thinking about in my head; so, Concrete Representative, Abstract. That's something I learned in my math classes in my teacher prep program. One of my professors was really good about showing us that." This Robin graduate went on to explain how she also referenced textbooks used in the mathematics methods course. In her words, "I referenced those [books] for fractions recently and I referenced them over Christmas break." The conceptual and structural coherence that Robin's faculty worked to build provided Robin candidates with a clear vision of teaching and learning and a set of teaching practices aligned with it that they used to guide and enact their teaching in their first years of their careers.

CONCLUSION

Our findings provide a portrait of elementary teacher candidates' learning experiences in their preparation programs. On the whole, candidates across the five programs in the DAI study reported having opportunities to build their knowledge of general instructional methods as well as methods for teaching diverse learners. In addition, candidates reported having opportunities to practice enacting ambitious teaching strategies in both mathematics and ELA, especially with elementary students in their student teaching placements. At the same time, we found some variation across the programs in candidates' opportunities to try out these strategies in their methods classes and to examine representations of ambitious instructional practices. Candidates across the programs also generally viewed their preparation programs as structurally and conceptually coherent. On average, they felt that their programs promoted a clear vision of teaching and learning that was shared across their preparation courses and elementary school placements.

Taken together, our findings indicate that the five different preparation programs provided candidates with a conceptual understanding of teaching and learning and offered them opportunities to build their knowledge of ambitious teaching practices and how to enact them. In the following chapters, we explore the different types of opportunities to learn offered by the programs that contributed to beginning teachers' instructional development and, specifically, their enactment of ambitious instructional practices in their first years of teaching.

CHAPTER 3

Beginning Teachers' Development of Ambitious Instructional Practices

Trajectories, Learning Opportunities, and Instructional Supports

As efforts to raise learning standards and hold educational systems accountable continue to drive educational policy in the United States, a broad consensus has emerged among educational researchers and policy makers that teacher quality is the most influential in-school factor affecting student learning.[1] In turn, teachers, including beginning teachers, are increasingly called on to teach in ways that foster students' deeper understanding of core disciplinary concepts and practices. Yet, ambitious instruction poses challenges for novice teachers, teacher educators, and K–12 schools alike. It requires that teachers plan intellectually demanding tasks; adapt their instruction in response to students' ideas, needs, and interests; and elicit and learn from multiple forms of evidence of student learning.[2]

This can be especially daunting for beginning elementary teachers, who typically teach multiple subjects. In addition, because ambitious instruction develops in and through the interactions between and among teachers' instructional goals, students' ideas, and the content being studied, it is not something that novice teachers can simply implement after reading about or observing it during teacher preparation or as they follow curricular guidelines in the schools where they begin their careers. Beginning teachers must build both their skills utilizing ambitious pedagogical strategies and their pedagogical reasoning, or the knowledge of when, how, and why to use the strategies with their particular students.[3]

Ensuring that novice teachers can teach ambitiously from day one thus raises several critical questions. For example, how do beginning teachers develop ambitious instructional practices? Several large-scale studies indicate that novice teachers' effectiveness, as measured by student achievement scores, steadily increases across their first years of teaching.[4] We currently know less, however, about how beginning teachers' actual teaching practices evolve during these years. Do novice teachers develop some ambitious practices more readily at the start of their careers? Do some practices remain more challenging for them? What types of learning opportunities and instructional supports can teacher education programs and K–12 schools provide to assist beginning teachers in developing these practices?

This chapter explores these questions through a series of analyses using survey and observational data from the Development of Ambitious Instruction (DAI) study. We collected these data from surveying and observing beginning teachers as they completed student teaching and throughout their first two years of teaching. The first analysis examines the teachers' Protocol for Language Arts Teaching Observation (PLATO) scores in mathematics and English language arts (ELA) to identify which instructional practices they were able to enact more (or less) ambitiously during their first two years. While we find that the novices' instruction improved between year 1 and year 2, the improvement was small and occurred in relation to some practices but not others. We then present analyses that examine the teacher preparation learning opportunities and school-based instructional supports that contributed to the beginning teachers' enactment of ambitious instruction in mathematics and ELA in their first two years.

In each case, we also consider novice teachers' individual characteristics as well as the school contexts in which they begin their teaching careers. We find that different opportunities and supports mattered across year 1 and year 2 and across mathematics and ELA. Teachers' individual characteristics and their contexts also seemed to influence the quality of their mathematics and ELA instruction, again, in different ways. Taken together, the analyses illuminate the pattern of beginning teachers' development of ambitious instructional practices and provide insights into how teacher education and induction programs might better support it across and within these two subject areas.

PLATO AS A MEASURE OF AMBITIOUS INSTRUCTION

As noted in chapter 1, in all three analyses we present here, we used PLATO to assess the ambitiousness of the instruction that we observed. Pamela Grossman and her colleagues developed PLATO to measure the ambitiousness of instruction in ELA.[5] Given our interest in understanding how elementary teachers develop ambitious instructional practices across the subjects they teach, we used a version of PLATO developed by Julie Cohen for assessing the quality of mathematics as well as ELA lessons.[6] The instructional domains PLATO delineates have been a focus of recent mathematics education reform efforts in the United States.[7] PLATO thus represents a useful, policy-relevant measure of instructional quality in both ELA and mathematics.

PLATO assesses the ambitiousness of teachers' instructional practices in four domains: instructional scaffolding, disciplinary demand, representations and organization of content, and classroom environment. It further delineates dimensions within each domain. For example, the instructional scaffolding domain includes the dimensions of modeling, conceptual strategy use and instruction, procedural strategy use and instruction, and feedback. Table 3.1 describes each dimension

TABLE 3.1 An overview of the PLATO classroom observation instrument domains and dimensions

Domain: representations and organization of content	
Representation of content	Representation of content is the element that focuses on the teacher's ability and accuracy in representing content to students through effective and meaningful explanations, examples, and analogies, along with the conceptual richness of the teacher's instructional explanations. At the lowest level, the teacher may introduce ideas but either does not provide any examples or explanations or provides incorrect examples or explanations. At the highest level, the teacher provides clear and nuanced explanations and helps students distinguish between different but related ideas, and the instruction focuses on conceptual understanding of disciplinary content.
Purpose	Purpose attempts to capture both the coherence of the lesson around a communicated objective (internal learning goal) and the position of the lesson within a larger context (situated learning goal). The internal learning goal speaks to lesson structure and the relevance of classroom activities toward meeting a learning goal identified by the teacher. The situated learning goal speaks to the future relevance to motivate the students to engage with the task at hand. The element focuses on whether the purpose of the lesson is made explicit by the teacher and is reflected in the activities undertaken by the class. At the highest level, purpose is clearly articulated, the lesson activities directly address and make progress toward the stated purpose, and the teacher or students check their progress toward achieving the purpose during and at the end of the lesson.
Domain: disciplinary demand	
Intellectual challenge	Intellectual challenge focuses on the intellectual rigor of the activities in which students engage during the instructional segment. Activities with high intellectual challenge ask students to engage in analytic or inferential thinking. Activities with low challenge, in contrast, require students to engage only in recall or rote thinking. Intellectual challenge also depends on the level of analytic or inferential thinking demanded by the questions asked by the teacher during class activities.
Classroom discourse	Classroom discourse focuses on the opportunities students have for extended content-related talk with the teacher or among peers and the extent to which the teacher and other students pick up on, build on, and clarify each other's ideas. At the low end, the teacher does the majority of the talking, and if student talk is present, the teacher and students do not build on previous responses; rather, the talk is disconnected. At the highest level, students engage in elaborated, coherent, and focused discussions in which the teacher and other students build on each other's contributions and prompt each other to clarify and specify their ideas.

TABLE 3.1 *continued*

Text-based instruction (ELA only)	Text-based instruction captures the degree to which students engage in ELA activities and discourse grounded in authentic texts. This includes when students engage with and/or produce authentic texts, such as published material, student-generated work, films, music, or artworks. At the high end, the teacher provides activities or opportunities for discussing or producing texts that require students to analyze specific features of a text to build their understanding of how to approach texts in general or how to attend to issues of writing craft, style, or genre in their writing. At the low end, there are no or minimal opportunities for students to read, discuss, or produce authentic texts.
Domain: instructional scaffolding	
Modeling and use of models	Modeling and use of models focuses on the degree to which a teacher visibly enacts strategies, skills, and processes targeted in the lesson to guide students' work before or while they complete the task, the extent to which they are analyzed or not, and whether they are used to illustrate for students what constitutes good work on a given task. The teacher might, for example, model discussion strategies or conduct a think-aloud on how to identify themes in ELA or, in mathematics, convert fractions to decimals as she explains her thinking and highlights the importance of place value. This element also includes the use of models to support students in completing the task at hand. At the high end, the teacher decomposes specific features of the strategy, skill, or process by using modeling or models to provide detailed instruction. At the low end, the teacher may simply refer to a model, without using it to provide instruction in the task at hand or to visibly enact the targeted strategies, skills, or processes.
Conceptual strategy use and instruction	Strategy use and instruction focuses on the teacher's ability to teach strategies and skills that support students in developing as readers, writers, and mathematicians. Conceptual strategies are methods or ways to approach academic tasks that can be used flexibly. Conceptual strategy instruction teaches students how to systematically reason and make sense of academic tasks and may help students complete such tasks as reading for meaning, generating ideas for writing, understanding why a mathematical procedure works, or comparing multiple solution methods. The teacher can use a variety of methods for teaching strategies, including providing opportunities for guided practice. At the high end, teachers provide explicit and detailed instruction about conceptual strategies that include how and why to use them. At the low end, where strategy instruction is minimal or insufficient, teachers may refer to conceptual strategies but without discussing why or when to use them.

Continued

TABLE 3.1 *continued*

Procedural strategy use and instruction	Procedural strategy instruction focuses on the teaching of rules (e.g., grammar/spelling rules, definitions of parts of a story) or procedures (e.g., the steps of multidigit multiplication). The teacher can use a variety of methods for teaching strategies, including providing opportunities for guided practice. At the high end, teachers provide explicit and detailed instruction about procedural strategies that include how and why to use them. At the low end, where strategy instruction is minimal or insufficient, teachers may refer to procedural strategies but without discussing why or when to use them.
Feedback	Feedback focuses on the quality of feedback provided in response to student application of disciplinary skills, concepts, or strategies. Feedback includes comments on the quality or nature of student work as well as suggestions for how students can improve the quality of their work. At the high end, feedback is specific and targets the skills at the heart of the activity. The feedback helps students understand the quality of their work and helps students better perform the task at hand by addressing substantive elements of the task. At the low end, feedback consists of vague comments that are not clearly anchored in student work, and suggestions for improvement tend to be procedural (i.e., focused on the instructions for the activity rather than the skills or knowledge that students are applying).
Domain: classroom environment	
Behavior management	Behavior management focuses on the degree to which behavior management facilitates academic work and is concerned with behavioral norms and consequences. This component does not presume that an ideal classroom is a quiet and controlled one. The key question is whether student behavior is appropriate for the task at hand; an "orderly" classroom will look different during a lecture than it would during small-group work.
Time management	Time management focuses on the amount of time students are engaged in content-focused activity. It looks at the teacher's efficient organization of classroom routines and materials to ensure that little class time is lost and that instructional time is maximized. Periods of downtime may occur because of a lack of procedures for routines like getting into groups, passing out papers, or collecting work. In addition, behavior management issues may affect time management. For example, a teacher who spends a significant amount of whole-class activity addressing student misbehavior would be scored down on time management.

within the four domains. PLATO is designed to rate the quality of mathematics and ELA lessons in fifteen-minute segments. PLATO scores for each dimension within a segment range from 1 to 4 as follows:

- 1 indicates that there is almost no evidence of ambitious instruction.
- 2 indicates that there is limited evidence of ambitious instruction.
- 3 indicates that there is evidence of ambitious instruction with some weaknesses.
- 4 indicates that there is consistently strong evidence of ambitious instruction.

As it parses teaching into its constituent practices, PLATO illuminates the nuances of teachers' development of ambitious instruction;[8] it also provides fine-grained insights into how it can be supported.

PATTERNS OF BEGINNING TEACHERS' INSTRUCTIONAL DEVELOPMENT IN THEIR FIRST TWO YEARS

In this section, we examine patterns of beginning teachers' enactment of ambitious instructional practices in their first two years of teaching to identify which practices novice teachers enact more ambitiously from day one and which practices prove more challenging for them. Specifically, we examine changes in beginning elementary teachers' PLATO scores in mathematics and ELA between their first and second years of teaching for the three PLATO instructional domains (i.e., instructional scaffolding, disciplinary demand, representations and organization of content) and the classroom environment domain.

Analytic strategy

For this analysis, we drew on classroom observation data featuring 625 mathematics and ELA lessons collected from sixty-four elementary teachers whom we observed teach lessons in mathematics and ELA in their first and second years of teaching. We observed almost all the teachers teach three lessons of mathematics and/or three lessons of ELA. In a few cases, we were able to observe them teach mathematics or ELA only twice ($N = 6$).

We relied on a series of simple descriptive statistics to explore the beginning teachers' instructional development. First, we aggregated teachers' PLATO scores from the observation level to the year level by taking the average of each teacher's rating within a given subject, domain, and/or dimension across their observations within a given year. Then, to summarize growth across the first and second years of teaching, we calculated the difference in each teacher's average year 1 and year 2 rating, again within a given subject, domain, and/or dimension.

For example, to assess the extent to which teachers increased the quality of their instructional scaffolding in their mathematics lessons between year 1 and year 2, we (a) took the mean of each teacher's observation score in instructional scaffolding across their mathematics observations occurring in the first year; (b) took the mean of each teacher's observation score in instructional scaffolding across their mathematics observations occurring in the second year; (c) for each teacher, subtracted the first value from the second to calculate the observed change; and (d) took the mean of the observed change for mathematics in instructional scaffolding across all teachers in our sample. We assessed statistical significance using a one-sample *t*-test of whether the average change score was different from zero.[9] Because we have a relatively small sample size for this analysis compared to the number of variables we are interested in (i.e., eleven dimensions across each of two subjects for twenty-two total dimensions), we focus primarily on patterns in direction and magnitude.

Findings

Table 3.2 reports the findings of our analysis of the beginning teachers' year 1 and year 2 PLATO scores at the domain level. It also reports the year 1 overall composite measure that represents an average across

TABLE 3.2 Changes in beginning teachers' enactment of ambitious instruction at the domain level between year 1 and year 2

PLATO score	*ELA*			*Math*			*Difference*
	Year 1 mean	*Year 1 to 2 change*	*Effect size diff.*	*Year 1 mean*	*Year 1 to 2 change*	*Effect size diff.*	*ELA change less math change in raw units*
Composite	2.25	0.09**	0.33	2.23	0.10**	0.37	−0.01
	[0.28]	(0.03)		[0.26]	(0.03)		(0.05)
Instructional composite	1.94	0.08*	0.31	1.97	0.08*	0.29	0.01
	[0.29]	(0.03)		[0.24]	(0.04)		(0.05)
Instructional scaffolding	1.67	0.03	0.10	1.85	0.04	0.14	−0.01
	[0.24]	(0.04)		[0.24]	(0.04)		(0.06)
Disciplinary demand	1.96	0.12*	0.31	1.92	0.14**	0.33	−0.01
	[0.46]	(0.06)		[0.36]	(0.05)		(0.08)
Representations and organization of content	2.20	0.10*	0.28	2.14	0.06	0.17	0.04
	[0.39]	(0.05)		[0.29]	(0.04)		(0.06)
Classroom environment	3.16	0.11†	0.23	3.00	0.16**	0.34	−0.06
	[0.5]	(0.05)		[0.45]	(0.06)		(0.08)

Note: Year 1 standard deviations are in brackets, and the standard errors of the difference between year 1 and year 2 are in parentheses.

**$p < 0.01$, *$p < 0.05$, †$p < 0.10$ for t-test of whether estimates are significantly different from zero.

all four domains for each year, and an instructional domain composite measure that represents an average across the three instructional domains (i.e., instructional scaffolding, disciplinary demand, representations and organization of content) for each year.

As Table 3.2 indicates, on average, we find only limited evidence of ambitious teaching across the sixty-four beginning teachers in year 1 in both ELA and mathematics. The year 1 composite scores in both ELA

($M = 2.25$, $SD = .28$) and mathematics ($M = 2.23$; $SD = .26$) were in the low 2 range. When we look at the different domains, we find that the highest scores in ELA ($M = 3.16$, $SD = .5$) and mathematics ($M = 3.00$, $SD = .45$) were in the classroom environment domain. Even in year 1, novice teachers, on average, were able to manage student behavior and instructional time in ways that facilitated their students' engagement in learning activities. In year 1, the beginning teachers struggled, however, to teach ambitiously in the instructional domains. Across both subjects, the highest scores in these domains were in representations and organization of content (ELA = 2.20; mathematics = 2.14), while the lowest scores were in instructional scaffolding (ELA = 1.67; mathematics = 1.85).

We did find that the beginning teachers, on average, improved the overall quality of their instruction between year 1 and year 2 in both ELA and mathematics. The overall ELA and mathematics composite scores improved by 0.09 points and 0.10 points, respectively, while the ELA and mathematics instructional composite scores both improved by 0.08 points. While the improvement across these measures is small, it is statistically significant. The changes in the overall ELA and mathematics composite scores were significant at the $p < 0.01$ level while the changes in the ELA and mathematics instructional composite scores were significant at the $p < 0.05$ level.

Within the instructional domains, we also find small but statistically significant growth in both ELA (.12 improvement points) and mathematics (.14 improvement points) in the disciplinary demand domain. The changes in the ELA disciplinary demand scores were significant at the $p < 0.05$ level, while the changes in the mathematics disciplinary demand scores were significant at the $p < 0.01$ level. We also find a small but significant improvement (.10 improvement points) in the representations and organization of content domain in ELA. The changes in the ELA representations scores were significant at the $p < 0.05$ level. We find no significant growth in either subject in the instructional scaffolding domain.

Our analysis of the year 1 and year 2 scores at the domain level thus indicates that in both ELA and mathematics the beginning teachers, on average, improved their skills in raising the rigor of the tasks in which they engaged their students. They also improved their skills in making ELA concepts and procedures more accessible to their students.

Our analysis of the novice teachers' PLATO scores at the dimension level provides more insight into the instructional practices they were able to enact more (or less) ambitiously within the PLATO instructional domains. Table 3.3 reports the mean PLATO dimension scores for year 1 and the change in these dimension scores between year 1 and year 2.

TABLE 3.3 Changes in beginning teachers' enactment of ambitious instruction at the dimension level between year 1 and year 2

PLATO score	*ELA*			*Math*			
	Year 1 mean	*Year 1 to 2 change*	*Effect size diff.*	*Year 1 mean*	*Year 1 to 2 change*	*Effect size diff.*	*ELA change less math change in raw units*
Instructional scaffolding: modeling	1.67	0.04	0.09	1.99	0.02	0.05	0.02
	[0.4]	(0.06)		[0.42]	(0.08)		(0.1)
Instructional scaffolding: conceptual strategy	1.34	0.13*	0.32	1.37	0.03	0.08	0.09
	[0.32]	(0.06)		[0.35]	(0.06)		(0.09)
Instructional scaffolding: procedural strategy	1.45	−0.04	−0.08	1.94	0.0	0	−0.04
	[0.34]	(0.06)		[0.39]	(0.09)		(0.11)
Instructional scaffolding: feedback	2.22	−0.03	−0.12	2.09	0.1**	0.41	−0.12*
	[0.25]	(0.04)		[0.19]	(0.03)		(0.05)

Continued

TABLE 3.3 *continued*

PLATO score	*ELA*			*Math*			
Disciplinary demand: intellectual challenge	1.91	0.21**	0.48	1.97	0.2***	0.48	0.0
	[0.48]	(0.07)		[0.37]	(0.05)		(0.08)
Disciplinary demand: classroom discourse	1.88	0.03	0.06	1.88	0.07	0.16	−0.04
	[0.41]	(0.06)		[0.42]	(0.07)		(0.09)
Disciplinary demand: text-based instruction	2.09	0.14	0.22				
	[0.63]	(0.09)					
Representations and organization of content: representation of content	2.13	0.06	0.14	2.11	0.07	0.17	−0.01
	[0.44]	(0.06)		[0.4]	(0.06)		(0.09)
Representations and organization of content: purpose	2.28	0.14*	0.34	2.16	0.05	0.11	0.1
	[0.46]	(0.07)		[0.35]	(0.05)		(0.09)
Classroom environment: behavior management	3.33	0.08	0.15	3.27	0.13*	0.23	−0.04
	[0.6]	(0.07)		[0.52]	(0.06)		(0.09)
Classroom environment: time management	2.98	0.13*	0.26	2.72	0.2**	0.39	−0.07
	[0.49]	(0.06)		[0.53]	(0.07)		(0.09)

Note: Year 1 standard deviations are in brackets and the standard errors of the difference between Year 1 and Year 2 are in parentheses. ***$p<0.001$, **$p<0.01$, *$p<0.05$, †$p<0.10$ for t-test of whether estimates of change are significantly different from zero.

As Table 3.3 shows, the beginning teachers, on average, improved their classroom management skills between year 1 and year 2, especially in mathematics. They demonstrated statistically significant growth in managing both student behavior and time. Within the instructional domains, the beginning teachers made small but statistically significant improvements in both ELA (.21 improvement points) and mathematics (.20 improvement points) in the intellectual challenge dimension. In ELA, the beginning teachers, on average, also improved their skills in the purpose dimension.

Summarizing beginning teachers' pattern of instructional development

Our analysis of the beginning teachers' year 1 and year 2 PLATO scores highlights several dimensions of their development of ambitious instructional practices. First, the analysis shows that the novice teachers, on average, had strong classroom management skills and that they improved their skills at managing time in both ELA and mathematics between year 1 and year 2. Classroom management skills are foundational to ambitious instruction. Engaging students in intellectually challenging tasks that build their knowledge of disciplinary concepts and practices requires establishing and reinforcing norms and routines that promote the behaviors appropriate for each task at hand and that keep students focused on learning. Beginning teachers can struggle to establish these norms and routines, especially in their first year of teaching. These struggles are one reason many novice teachers leave the profession. Our analysis indicates that on average, the beginning teachers in our study started their teaching careers possessing the foundational management skills to teach ambitiously.

At the same time, our analysis also shows that the novice teachers struggled to enact ambitious instructional practices in both ELA and mathematics. It is important to note that earlier studies that have used PLATO have found that even experienced teachers struggle to teach ambitiously across the different domains and dimensions. Pamela Grossman and her colleagues used a version of PLATO without the representations and organization of content domain to analyze ELA lessons from the Measures of Effective Teaching project, which collected observations of mostly ELA and mathematics lessons from three thousand teachers. The average composite score was 2.51, with the highest mean domain score, 3.61, in the classroom environment domain. The mean score in the disciplinary demand domain was 2.25 and only 1.64 in the instructional scaffolding domain.[10] Similarly, Julie Cohen's analysis of instructional scaffolding in the mathematics lessons of 103 elementary teachers of mixed experience levels found that roughly two-thirds of the teachers received a 1 for conceptual strategy instruction, a 1 or 2 for procedural strategy instruction, and a 1 or 2 for modeling on the PLATO four-point scale.[11] The PLATO scores for the beginning teachers in our study broadly compare to these scores, though they are lower in ELA in disciplinary demand and somewhat lower in the classroom environment domain.

Despite how challenging teaching ambitiously is for all teachers, beginning teachers in our study did improve their instruction in some domains and dimensions. In both ELA and mathematics, they demonstrated growth in the disciplinary demand domain. Much of this growth occurred in the intellectual challenge dimension. We did not find statistically significant changes in either subject in the other dimensions of disciplinary demand: classroom discourse (ELA or mathematics) or text-based instruction (ELA). In ELA, the novices also improved their skills in representations and organization of content, with much of this growth demonstrated in the purpose dimension. These scores indicate that though the beginning teachers, on average, engaged students in ELA and mathematics tasks that were largely rote or recall, in year 2 they more often engaged students in analysis, interpretation, or idea generation for some portion of these tasks. In ELA, they also improved in communicating learning goals that supported their students' ELA development.

Our analysis suggests that intellectual challenge and purpose may be dimensions in which beginning teachers can more readily develop their skills during their first years of teaching. Unlike classroom discourse—a dimension of disciplinary demand that involves teachers facilitating discussions in which they respond in the moment to students' ideas—these dimensions more closely reflect the tasks that teachers assign. Teachers often select these tasks from the curricular and instructional materials that schools and districts make available and sometimes mandate that they use. Novice teachers expend considerable effort learning how to teach with these materials.[12] As they become more familiar with these materials, they may be better able both to establish and maintain the intellectual rigor of the tasks they assign and to communicate their learning goals.

In contrast, facilitating ambitious classroom discourse might take more time and require more explicit support for beginning teachers to cultivate. There is evidence that mentor teachers and instructional coaches, when they target their work with novice teachers on specific discussion practices, can provide such support.[13] For their part, teacher educators can help preservice teachers build their discussion skills by providing them opportunities in methods courses and field experiences to try out facilitating classroom talk in which students clarify, evaluate, and expand on their own and each other's ideas as they engage with disciplinary content through academic tasks.[14]

While the beginning teachers developed their skills in increasing the rigor and clarifying the goals of the tasks they assigned their students, we found very little growth in their enactment of instructional scaffolding practices in either ELA or mathematics. Their scores in modeling, conceptual strategy instruction, and procedural strategy instruction, especially in ELA, were among the lowest across the eleven PLATO dimensions. Instructional scaffolding, as measured by PLATO, is consistently associated with positive student learning outcomes.[15] Yet, our analysis indicates that novice teachers are not likely to develop ambitious scaffolding practices simply as a result of gaining more teaching experience. Findings from other studies that show how experienced teachers also tend to employ these practices in rule-bound rather than adaptive ways further suggest that beginning teachers are likely to need considerably more support in this domain. Such support, in both teacher education programs and K–12 schools, will need to assist novice teachers in understanding how, when, and why to use models, teach strategies, and provide feedback to make disciplinary concepts and practices accessible to students in ways that elicit and expand their ideas.

Finally, we found mostly similar patterns of challenge and growth in mathematics and ELA between the first and second years of teaching. On the one hand, this highlights the difficulties ambitious instruction poses for beginning teachers in both subjects. On the other hand, the similarities in patterns also suggest that supporting novice teachers in cultivating more ambitious instructional practices in one subject might facilitate their enactment of these practices in another subject. Given persistent time and cost constraints faced by teacher preparation and K–12 schools, finding ways that leverage beginning teachers' learning in one subject for their learning in another subject holds some promise. At the same time, because ambitious instruction focuses on rigorous subject matter learning, it is also important to help elementary teachers understand when, how, and why to modify and adapt ambitious practices when they teach different subjects.

How opportunities to learn are associated with ambitious instruction in the first year

Our second analysis in this chapter examines the teacher preparation learning opportunities that contribute to beginning elementary teachers' skills enacting ambitious instruction in mathematics and ELA in their first year of teaching.[16] Research during the past decade shows that providing preservice teachers opportunities to build their content and content pedagogical knowledge can assist them in teaching ambitiously. Studies of practice-based teacher education programs, for example, document how opportunities for preservice teachers to decompose ambitious instructional practices into their component parts, analyze representations of these practices (e.g., unit plans or video-recorded lessons), and rehearse using them in methods classes with peers or small groups of students can assist first-year teachers' enactment of these strategies.[17] Because these studies typically focus on a small number of beginning teachers in a single program, it is difficult to assess which learning opportunities matter for novices across multiple programs.

To address this gap, other researchers have conducted large-scale studies of elementary teacher candidates' opportunities to learn in teacher preparation across multiple programs. These studies find that beginning teachers have greater impact on student learning if, as preservice teachers, they had opportunities in coursework to develop their content and pedagogical content knowledge and to engage in actual instructional practice (e.g., assessing students' ability to read aloud, analyzing student mathematics work) and if, as student teachers, they worked with instructionally effective cooperating teachers in well-managed schools.[18] These studies also indicate that the socioeconomic status of students and the academic performance of the schools where candidates student teach can influence their effectiveness as novice teachers. Few of these large-scale studies, however, have examined how teacher preparation learning opportunities are associated with beginning teachers' enactment of ambitious instructional practices.

Prior studies have also documented the importance of opportunities to learn general pedagogical strategies and strategies for teaching culturally diverse students. General pedagogical strategies include lesson planning, formative and summative student assessment, ways to facilitate group work, and ways to differentiate instruction.[19] Opportunities to learn these strategies are associated with elementary candidates' knowledge and first-year elementary teachers' effectiveness.[20] Similarly, studies have shown that opportunities to learn how to teach diverse students, including demonstrating high academic expectations for all students and promoting students' cultural competence, cultural integrity, and sociopolitical consciousness, can foster beginning teachers' development of culturally responsive teaching practices.[21] Few studies, though, have explored how opportunities to learn either general methods strategies or strategies for teaching diverse students relate to novice teachers' enactment of ambitious instruction.

Taken together, these studies identify several types of teacher preparation learning opportunities that might contribute to beginning teachers' enactment of ambitious instructional practices. We explore these opportunities in our analysis here. Because ambitious instruction requires that teachers skillfully plan for and facilitate students' engagement with disciplinary content in ways that are consistently rigorous and responsive to students' ideas and to the complexities of classroom interactions,[22] we also consider the influence that teachers' content knowledge for teaching, their teaching self-efficacy, and the characteristics of their teaching assignments have on their first-year instruction. Teachers with high levels of content knowledge for teaching and teaching self-efficacy have been found to be more likely to enact high-quality instruction,[23]and they are thereby more likely to promote student achievement in mathematics and ELA.[24] There is also some evidence that teachers' grade-level assignments are associated with the quality of their instruction. Pamela Grossman and her colleagues found, for example, that upper elementary ELA teachers (grades 4 and 5) had higher PLATO scores than middle and high school ELA teachers.[25]

Analytic strategy

For our analysis of opportunities to learn and first-year teachers' enactment of ambitious instruction, we draw on observations from eighty-three first-year teachers who participated in our study. We observed almost all these teachers teach three lessons of mathematics and/or ELA. In a few cases, we were able to observe them teach only two mathematics lessons ($N = 6$) and/or two ELA lessons ($N = 5$).

Table 3.4 summarizes the different factors we examined in our analysis of the quality of first-year teachers' instruction in our study. It also identifies the data sources we used to assess each. To assess how elementary candidate characteristics and learning experiences in teacher preparation were associated with first-year teachers' enactment of ambitious instructional practices, we ran a series of single-level, multiple linear regression analyses. We report the results of these analyses in Tables 3.5 and 3.6. Each regression model tested each of the four PLATO domains in mathematics and ELA as the outcome variables. The instructional composite was entered as a predictor variable. (See the methodological appendix for more information on our data sources and methods of analysis.)

Findings

Tables 3.5 and 3.6 present the four models predicting first-year teacher PLATO mathematics and ELA scores, respectively. In particular, the goodness-of-fit statistics (R^2) indicate that across all mathematics outcomes, predictor variables consistently explained more than 45 percent of the variability in the outcomes. The analysis shows that general pedagogical strategies played a central role in the extent to which the beginning teachers in our study enacted ambitious instructional practices in year 1. Novice teachers who reported having opportunities as preservice teachers to learn these strategies generally had higher PLATO scores in disciplinary demand and instructional scaffolding in both mathematics and ELA than teachers lacking such opportunities.

TABLE 3.4 Key constructs and data sources used in analyses of learning opportunities and first-year teachers' enactment of ambitious instruction

Teacher characteristics	*OTL+ in courses*	*OTL in student teaching*	*Program coherence*	*Teaching assignment; school characteristics*	*First-year teachers' enactment of ambitious instruction*
Content knowledge for teaching *Data Sources: Mathematical Knowledge for Teaching survey; Teaching Knowledge about Reading and Reading Practices* Mathematics and ELA teaching self-efficacy *Data Source: Elementary Teacher Candidate survey* Race/ethnicity, gender, SAT/ACT scores, and undergraduate GPA *Data Source: Elementary Teacher Candidate survey*	OTL general principles of instruction, OTL teaching diverse students *Data Source: Elementary Teacher Candidate survey*	Opportunities to observe, use, and receive feedback on ambitious instructional practices in mathematics and ELA *Data Source: Elementary Teacher Candidate survey*	Program coherence *Data Source: Elementary Teacher Candidate survey*	Teaching assignment *Data Source: First-Year Teacher survey* School Characteristics (i.e., percentage of students eligible for free/reduced-price lunch) *Data Source: Common Core of Data*	Enactment of ambitious instruction in mathematics and ELA *Data Source: Classroom observations using PLATO*

Note: +OTL = opportunities to learn.

TABLE 3.5 Linear regression models predicting first-year teachers' enactment of ambitious instructional practices in mathematics

	PLATO mathematics			
	Classroom environment	*Instructional scaffolding*	*Disciplinary demand*	*Representations of content*
	β (SE)	*β (SE)*	*β (SE)*	*β (SE)*
Teacher characteristics				
Gender (0 = female, 1 = male)	−0.01 (0.09)	−0.01 (0.10)	−0.03 (0.09)	0.10 (0.09)
Race (0 = white, 1 = Teacher of Color)	−0.11 (0.09)	−0.07 (0.10)	0.10 (0.09)	−0.06 (0.10)
Undergrad GPA	**−0.20* (0.09)**	**0.22* (0.10)**	0.11 (0.09)	**0.29* (0.10)**
SAT/ACT math percentile	0.03 (0.10)	<.01 (0.11)	0.01 (0.10)	0.05 (0.11)
Math knowledge for teaching	**−0.19+ (0.10)**	**0.27* (0.11)**	0.02 (0.10)	0.16 (0.10)
Self-efficacy re: teaching math	**0.28* (0.11)**	**−0.45* (0.11)**	−0.03 (0.10)	**−0.44* (0.11)**
First-year teaching assignment				
Upper elementary	**0.27* (0.09)**	−0.14 (0.10)	−0.05 (0.09)	**−0.29* (0.10)**
Free/reduced-price lunch percentage at FYT school	0.01 (0.09)	−0.10 (0.10)	**−0.31** (0.09)**	−0.04 (0.10)
PLATO				
PLATO predictor variable	**0.70* (0.08)**	**0.45* (0.09)**	**0.57* (0.08)**	**0.54* (0.09)**

Continued

TABLE 3.5 *continued*

	PLATO mathematics			
	Classroom environment	*Instructional scaffolding*	*Disciplinary demand*	*Representations of content*
Opportunities to learn (OTL)				
OTL general principles of instruction	−0.16 (0.09)	**0.26* (0.10)**	**0.26* (0.09)**	0.10 (0.10)
OTL strategies for teaching diverse students	**0.29* (0.10)**	**−0.40* (0.10)**	**−0.22* (0.09)**	**−0.26* (0.10)**
OTL math instructional strategies during student teaching	**−0.23* (0.09)**	**0.28* (0.10)**	<.01 (0.09)	**0.21* (0.10)**
R-squared	*0.56*	*0.46*	*0.54*	*0.46*

Note: Table 3.5 presents standardized coefficients, with standard errors in parentheses. Bolded values represent statistically significant effects. In model predicting classroom environment, *PLATO predictor variable* represents a PLATO mathematics instructional composite score that is the mean of scores on the three mathematics instructional domains; in the models predicting each of the three mathematics instructional domains, *PLATO predictor variable* represents the PLATO mathematics classroom environment score.

$+p < .10$, $^{*}p < .05.$, $^{**}p < .01$.

TABLE 3.6 Linear regression models predicting first-year teachers' enactment of ambitious instructional practices in ELA

	PLATO ELA			
	Classroom environment	*Instructional scaffolding*	*Disciplinary demand*	*Representations of content*
	β (SE)	*β (SE)*	*β (SE)*	*β (SE)*
Teacher characteristics				
Gender (0 = female, 1 = male)	0.13 (0.11)	−0.05 (0.11)	−0.05 (0.10)	−0.15 (0.11)
Race (0 = white, 1 = Teacher of Color)	**−0.22* (0.11)**	−0.05 (0.11)	0.14 (0.09)	**0.21+ (0.11)**
Undergrad GPA	0.07 (0.12)	**0.24* (0.12)**	**0.22* (0.10)**	**0.27* (0.12)**
SAT/ACT ELA percentile	0.02 (0.12)	0.08 (0.12)	−0.05 (0.10)	0.09 (0.11)
Reading knowledge score	−0.04 (0.12)	0.08 (0.12)	0.15 (0.10)	0.08 (0.12)
Self-efficacy re: teaching ELA	**0.21+ (0.12)**	−0.14 (0.12)	**−0.28* (0.10)**	−0.11 (0.12)
First-year teaching assignment				
Upper elementary	−0.04 (0.11)	−0.09 (0.11)	**0.25** (0.10)**	0.06 (0.11)
Free/reduced-price lunch percentage at FYT school	−0.13 (0.12)	**−0.23+ (0.12)**	**−0.33* (0.10)**	0.02 (0.11)

Continued

TABLE 3.6 *continued*

	PLATO ELA			
	Classroom environment	*Instructional scaffolding*	*Disciplinary demand*	*Representations of content*
PLATO				
PLATO predictor variable	**0.27* (0.12)**	0.08 (0.11)	**0.23* (0.10)**	**0.22+ (0.11)**
Opportunities to learn (OTL)				
OTL general principles of instruction	–0.06 (0.12)	**0.24* (0.12)**	**0.30* (0.10)**	0.16 (0.12)
OTL strategies for teaching diverse students	–0.08 (0.12)	–0.19 (0.12)	–0.05 (0.10)	0.04 (0.12)
OTL ELA instructional strategies during student teaching	–0.13 (0.12)	0.04 (0.12)	**–0.22* (0.10)**	–0.01 (0.12)
R-squared	*0.23*	*0.19*	*0.42*	*0.20*

Note: Table 3.6 presents standardized coefficients, with standard errors in parentheses. Bolded values represent statistically significant effects. In model predicting classroom environment, *PLATO predictor variable* represents a PLATO ELA instructional composite score that is the mean of scores on the three ELA instructional domains; in the models predicting each of the three ELA instructional domains, *PLATO predictor variable* represents the PLATO ELA classroom environment score.

$+p < .10$, $*p < .05$., $**p < .01$.

When teachers reported having opportunities to learn about, try out, and receive feedback on ambitious mathematics teaching strategies during student teaching, they generally received higher ratings than other first-year teachers for representations and organization of content and instructional scaffolding in mathematics. At the same time, when participants reported having opportunities to learn about, try out, and receive feedback on ambitious ELA teaching strategies during student teaching, they generally received lower ratings than other teachers for disciplinary demand in ELA.

We found that opportunities to learn strategies for working with diverse learners were positively associated with first-year teachers' scores in the PLATO classroom environment domain in mathematics. Learning these strategies in teacher preparation assisted first-year teachers in our study to manage student behavior and time in ways that facilitated students' engagement in academic tasks. At the same time, our analysis indicates that in mathematics, opportunities to learn these strategies in teacher preparation had significantly negative associations with the PLATO instructional domains. We found no significant associations with first-year teachers' enactment of ambitious practices in ELA, though, as in mathematics, the association with most of the PLATO domains were also negative.

It is notable that we also found that teachers who taught in high-poverty schools (as measured by the percentage of students eligible for free or reduced-price lunch) generally received lower ratings for disciplinary demand in both subjects and for instructional scaffolding in ELA. Taken together with the findings related to opportunities to learn strategies to work with diverse students, our findings indicate that first-year teachers in this project may have had difficulty integrating the strategies to teach diverse students they encountered in teacher preparation into their teaching practices in ways that engaged their students in intellectually challenging tasks, built on students' ideas, and developed students' understanding of disciplinary concepts and practices.

Our analysis shows that several teacher characteristics were significantly associated with first-year teachers' enactments of ambitious instructional practices. Higher undergraduate GPA was positively associated with first-year teachers having higher PLATO scores in all three ELA instructional domains and in instructional scaffolding and representations and organization of content in mathematics. Similarly, novices' mathematical knowledge for teaching was positively associated with their enactment of instructional scaffolding practices in mathematics. At the same time, higher GPAs and scores in mathematical knowledge for teaching were associated with lower classroom environment scores in mathematics. We did not find significant associations with any ELA ambitious practices and the measure we used to assess our participants' knowledge for teaching ELA.

Our findings regarding teaching self-efficacy in ELA and mathematics were also somewhat mixed. In the present analysis, we assessed teaching self-efficacy while the beginning teachers were still enrolled in their teacher preparation programs. Our analysis indicates that elementary candidates' teaching self-efficacy was positively associated with their PLATO scores in classroom environment, in both subjects, though this association was only marginally statistically significant in ELA. This aligns with findings from our first analysis that indicate that the novice teachers in our study, on average, entered teaching with strong classroom management skills. On the other hand, the candidates' teaching self-efficacy was negatively associated with their PLATO scores in instructional scaffolding and representations and organization of content in both subjects, and with disciplinary demand in ELA.

Finally, we found that the beginning teachers in our study who taught in grades 3–5 during their first year of teaching generally received higher PLATO ratings than teachers who taught in grades K–2 for classroom environment in mathematics and disciplinary demand in ELA, but lower ratings for representations and organization of content in mathematics. The ELA result suggests that the K–2 teachers tended to focus more on discrete and less demanding reading skills. The mathematics finding may be related to upper elementary mathematics content being more challenging to teach than lower elementary mathematics content and upper elementary teachers lacking sufficient mathematical content knowledge.

Summarizing factors associated with first-year teachers' instructional practices

The finding that opportunities to learn general teaching practices are associated with higher PLATO scores in mathematics and ELA is consistent with conceptual arguments about the value of general methods courses.[26] They indicate that first-year teachers strongly benefit when they have opportunities during teacher preparation to acquire knowledge about general principles and theories of instruction and to learn to plan lessons and units, facilitate group work, and foster student engagement and motivation. In particular, candidates who report having opportunities to learn general methods in their teacher preparation courses are more likely than other novice teachers to maintain the rigor of learning tasks they assign and to employ strategies, models, and feedback to foster students' understanding of disciplinary concepts and practices in both mathematics and ELA.

Our second main finding provides evidence that beginning teachers benefit from being able to try out and receive feedback in their student teaching placements on such mathematics strategies as designing tasks requiring high levels of cognitive demand, differentiating instruction, making connections to students' prior mathematical knowledge, identifying and responding to student thinking, and facilitating classroom discussion. These results are consistent with other research indicating that clinical placements can serve as key sites for novice teacher development.[27]

The negative association between opportunities to learn, try out, and receive feedback on ambitious ELA strategies during student teaching and disciplinary demand deserves further explanation. The disciplinary demand factor addresses the cognitive demand of the activities that teachers assign to their students, the quality of classroom discussions, and, in ELA, the use of authentic texts. The negative association we find suggests that first-year teachers in our study may have struggled to achieve a balance between enacting school and district ELA curricula and implementing ambitious practices.

The mixed results for learning opportunities related to teaching diverse students also warrant further discussion. Recent studies of efforts to support teachers enacting ambitious teaching practices with diverse students have found that both beginning and experienced teachers find this difficult and often do not even attempt to integrate students' cultural identities and the funds of knowledge students bring with them from their homes and communities into their teaching of academic content.[28] Studies of practice-based teacher education and justice-oriented teacher preparation have shown how providing learning opportunities and tools to build novices' capacity and commitment to eliciting and utilizing students' ideas as critical resources in their teaching can assist beginning teachers with this integration.[29] Our findings point to the critical importance of building on and expanding these efforts across teacher education and induction programs.

Finally, with regard to the negative association between teaching self-efficacy and PLATO scores in both subjects, we interpret this finding to mean that teacher candidates in this study generally had high levels of teaching self-efficacy and were not fully cognizant of how challenging it can be, especially as novice teachers, to enact ambitious practices in mathematics and ELA. The findings suggest that teacher preparation programs might consider how they can assist teacher candidates not only in employing these practices in courses and student teaching, but also in learning how to make sense of and address the challenges that arise when they do so.

HOW OPPORTUNITIES TO LEARN ARE ASSOCIATED WITH AMBITIOUS INSTRUCTION IN THE SECOND YEAR

In our first analysis above, we found that the novice teachers in the DAI study did, overall, teach more ambitiously in their second year of teaching. In this section, we explore the opportunities to learn in teacher preparation that might support this development. Specifically, we examine how elementary teacher candidates' opportunities to learn general pedagogical strategies, strategies for working with diverse learners, and ambitious strategies in ELA and mathematics were associated with second-year teachers' enactment of ambitious instruction in ELA and mathematics when accounting for these teachers' PLATO scores in ELA and mathematics, respectively, as first-year teachers. In particular, we explore second-year teachers' PLATO scores in ELA and mathematics for the three instructional domains (i.e., instructional scaffolding, disciplinary demand, representations and organization of content) and the classroom environment domain while taking account of their scores as first-year teachers in each of these domains.

Analytic strategy

For our analysis of opportunities to learn and second-year teachers' enactment of ambitious instruction, we draw on observations from sixty second-year teachers who participated in our study. We observed all sixty of these teachers teach two to three mathematics lessons in both their first and second years of teaching, and we observed fifty-six of them teach two to three ELA lessons in both their first year and their second year.

Table 3.4 provides information about the different factors we examined in our analysis of the quality of second-year teachers' instruction in our study and the data sources we used to assess each factor. In contrast to the first-year teacher PLATO analyses, based on results from factor analysis, we changed the predictor variable for strategies for teaching diverse students into two variables: strategies for teaching diverse students and strategies for addressing equity. We also added a predictor variable for program coherence, and based on results from factor analysis, we created two program coherence variables: program coherence I and program coherence II. (See the methodological appendix for more information on our data sources and methods of analysis.)

To assess how elementary candidate characteristics and learning experiences in teacher preparation were associated with second-year teachers' enactment of ambitious instructional practices, we ran a series of single-level, multiple linear regression analyses. We report the results of these analyses in Tables 3.7 and 3.8. Each regression model tested each of the four PLATO domains as the outcome variables.

Findings

Tables 3.7 and 3.8 present several models predicting second-year teachers' PLATO ELA and mathematics scores, respectively, while accounting for first-year teachers' PLATO scores. The analysis shows that learning opportunities during teacher preparation contributed to teachers' enactment of ambitious instructional practices in year 2 when taking account of their implementation of ambitious instruction in year 1. In particular, the goodness of fit statistics (R^2) indicate that across all outcomes, predictor variables consistently explained more than 50 percent of the variability in the outcomes.

In ELA, beginning teachers who perceived high levels of program coherence (i.e., the program coherence II variable) and who reported having opportunities to learn, try out, and receive feedback on ambitious ELA instructional strategies during clinical placements generally had higher PLATO ELA scores in representations and organization of content. In addition, novices who reported having opportunities to

TABLE 3.7 Linear regression models predicting second-year teachers' enactment of ambitious instructional practices in ELA when accounting for their enactment of such practices in their first year

	PLATO ELA			
	Classroom environment	*Instructional scaffolding*	*Disciplinary demand*	*Representations of content*
	β (SE)	*β (SE)*	*β (SE)*	*β (SE)*
Teacher characteristics				
Gender (0 = female, 1 = male)	−0.060 (0.180)	−0.193 (0.135)	−0.291 (0.179	−0.183 (0.167)
Race (0 = white, 1 = Teacher of Color)	0.085 (0.171)	−0.31 (0.128)	0.139 (0.169)	−0.164 (0.158)
Undergrad GPA	**−0.441* (0.178)**	−0.013 (0.135)	0.152 (0.178)	−0.001 (0.169)
SAT/ACT ELA percentile	0.003 (0.003)	0.002 (0.002)	0.002 (0.003)	0.000 (0.003)
Self-efficacy re: teaching ELA	**−0.085+ (0.050)**	0.026 (0.036)	−0.036 (0.050)	0.004 (0.045)
First-year teaching assignment				
Upper elementary	**0.226* (0.092)**	0.010 (0.071)	**0.189+ (0.100)**	**0.150+ (0.088)**
Free/reduced-price lunch percentage at second-year teacher (SYT) school	−0.253 (0.159)	**−0.224+ (0.123)**	0.237 (0.189)	−0.206 (0.146)
PLATO				
PLATO predictor variable	**0.703** (0.108)**	**0.360* (0.150)**	**0.275* (0.132)**	**0.405** (0.110)**

Continued

TABLE 3.7 *continued*

	PLATO ELA			
	Classroom environment	*Instructional scaffolding*	*Disciplinary demand*	*Representations of content*
Opportunities to learn (OTL)				
OTL general principles of instruction	**0.105* (0.045)**	0.028 (0.035)	0.036 (0.046)	–0.024 (0.045)
OTL strategies for teaching diverse students	0.073 (0.057)	0.013 (0.044)	0.023 (0.060)	–0.008 (0.055)
OTL strategies for addressing equity	–0.026 (0.048)	0.044 (0.036)	0.043 (0.048)	0.058 (0.046)
OTL ELA instructional strategies during courses/ student teaching	–0.090 (0.058)	–0.072 (0.045)	–0.029 (0.059)	**–0.135* (0.055)**
Program coherence I	0.016 (0.073)	–0.036 (0.054)	0.048 (0.075)	–0.099 (0.067)
Program coherence II	0.003 (0.057)	0.016 (0.044)	0.024 (0.060)	**0.103+ (0.055)**
OTL ELA instructional strategies during student teaching	0.006 (0.061)	0.047 (0.047)	–0.026 (0.060)	**0.134* (0.059)**
R-squared	*0.83*	*0.59*	*0.64*	*0.65*

Note: Table 3.7 presents standardized coefficients, with standard errors in parentheses. Bolded values represent statistically significant effects. In these models, *PLATO predictor variable* represents the teacher's PLATO score for a given domain during their first year of teaching.

+$p < .10$, *$p < .05$., **$p < .01$.

TABLE 3.8 Linear regression models predicting second-year teachers' enactment of ambitious instructional practices in mathematics when accounting for their enactment of such practices in their first year

	PLATO mathematics			
	Classroom environment	*Instructional scaffolding*	*Disciplinary demand*	*Representations of content*
	β (SE)	*β (SE)*	*β (SE)*	*β (SE)*
Teacher characteristics				
Gender (0 = female, 1 = male)	**−0.43+ (0.22)**	−0.160 (0.146)	0.054 (0.094)	0.157 (0.177)
Race (0 = white, 1 = Teacher of Color)	−0.22 (0.21)	**0.248+ (0.139)**	0.129 (0.087)	0.231 (0.171)
Undergrad GPA	−0.147 (0.22)	−0.240 (0.156)	−0.005 (0.095)	−0.165 (0.180)
SAT/ACT math percentile	0.00 (0.003)	0.001 (0.002)	**0.003* (0.001)**	0.001 (0.003)
Self-efficacy re: teaching math	−0.003 (0.049)	−0.003 (0.049)	−0.001 (0.030)	0.005 (0.058)
First-year teaching assignment				
Upper elementary	0.167 (0.111)	0.020 (0.073)	0.066 (0.047)	**0.152+ (0.088)**
Free/reduced-price lunch percentage at SYT school	−0.211 (0.205)	0.106 (0.141)	0.113 (0.096)	0.223 (0.170)
PLATO				
PLATO predictor variable	**0.569** (0.129)**	**0.608** (0.182)**	**0.206** (0.07)**	**0.612** (0.160)**

Continued

TABLE 3.8 *continued*

	PLATO mathematics			
	Classroom environment	*Instructional scaffolding*	*Disciplinary demand*	*Representations of content*
Opportunities to learn (OTL)				
OTL general principles of instruction	0.077 (0.058)	−0.055 (0.041)	−0.006 (0.025)	−0.035 (0.046)
OTL strategies for teaching diverse students	0.055 (0.074)	**0.105+ (0.053)**	−0.015 (0.031)	0.059 (0.059)
OTL strategies for addressing equity	−0.006 (0.067)	−0.028 (0.044)	0.022 (0.029)	0.000 (0.053)
OTL math instructional strategies during courses/student teaching	−0.102 (0.070)	−0.058 (0.047)	−0.018 (0.030)	−0.008 (0.056)
Program coherence I	−0.052 (0.104)	0.072 (0.068)	−0.030 (0.044)	−0.062 (0.082)
Program coherence II	−0.012 (0.080)	−0.045 (0.052)	0.011 (0.034)	0.057 (0.063)
OTL math instructional strategies during student teaching	0.084 (0.074)	−0.030 (0.049)	−0.014 (0.031)	0.014 (0.058)
R-squared	*0.67*	*0.58*	*0.65*	*0.58*

Note: Table 3.8 presents standardized coefficients, with standard errors in parentheses. Bolded values represent statistically significant effects. In these models, *PLATO predictor variable* represents the teacher's PLATO score for a given domain during their first year of teaching.
$+p < .10$, $*p < .05.$, $**p < .01$.

learn general pedagogical strategies generally had higher PLATO ELA scores in classroom environment. At the same time, beginning teachers who reported opportunities to learn ambitious ELA strategies in coursework generally had lower PLATO ELA scores in representations and organization of content.

Second-year teachers who taught in grades 3–5 (as opposed to grades K–2) generally had higher PLATO ELA scores in representations and organization of content, disciplinary demand, and classroom environment. However, some teacher and school characteristics had negative associations with PLATO ELA scores. Second-year teachers with relatively higher levels of ELA teaching self-efficacy and relatively higher grade point averages generally had lower PLATO ELA scores in the classroom environment. Further, second-year teachers working in schools that served relatively higher percentages of students eligible for free or reduced-price lunch generally had lower scores in instructional scaffolding.

In mathematics, second-year teachers who reported having opportunities to learn about strategies for teaching diverse learners generally had higher PLATO mathematics scores in instructional scaffolding. Further, novices who taught in grades 3–5 generally had higher PLATO mathematics scores in representations and organization of content than those who taught in grades K-2. With regard to teacher characteristics, compared with other second-year teachers those with higher SAT/ACT scores generally had higher PLATO mathematics scores in disciplinary demand, Teachers of Color generally had higher PLATO mathematics scores in instructional scaffolding, and male teachers generally had higher PLATO mathematics scores in classroom environment.

Summarizing factors associated with second-year teachers' instructional practices

In ELA, we found that beginning teachers are more likely to receive high ratings for representations and organization of content during their second year of teaching (taking account of their first-year scores) when they report having opportunities to learn, try out, and receive feedback on ambitious ELA instructional strategies during clinical placements. In their second year, these teachers were more likely to develop their ability to make the purpose of a given lesson explicit and accurately represent ELA content. These results align with other studies demonstrating that clinical placements often strongly influence novice teacher development.[30] The finding that program coherence was positively associated with second-year teachers' ratings for representations and organization of content in ELA during their second year is similarly consistent with prior research on the important role that coherence can play in beginning teachers' instructional development.[31]

We reported a negative association between opportunities to learn about ambitious ELA instructional strategies in courses and other preparation program settings (e.g., examining such strategies in videos or written cases and trying them with peers in methods courses) and representations and organization of content in ELA. We interpret this to mean that such experiences were much less salient for second-year teachers in our sample (with regard to instructional improvement) compared with opportunities during student teaching to learn about, try out, and receive feedback on these strategies during student teaching.

We also found that teaching in upper elementary grades as a second-year teacher was linked to higher PLATO ELA scores in disciplinary demand, representations and organization of content, and classroom environment. In other words, second-year teachers in grades 3–5 were more likely to receive higher ratings than teachers in grades K–2 in (a) engaging their students in analytic and inferential thinking during ELA instruction, (b) making the purpose of a given lesson clear and accurately representing ELA content, and (c) managing time and student behavior effectively. This may reflect a focus in grades K–2 on more discrete and less demanding reading skills.

Our finding about opportunities to learn general pedagogical practices indicates that second-year teachers are more likely to receive high ratings for their ELA classroom environment skills (i.e., time and behavior management) when they have opportunities during teacher preparation to acquire knowledge about general principles and theories of instruction and to learn generic skills such as planning lessons and units, facilitating group work, and fostering student engagement and motivation. In contrast, second-year teachers with higher levels of ELA teaching self-efficacy and higher undergraduate grade point averages generally had lower ELA classroom environment scores. We interpret this to mean that second-year teachers who performed academically at high levels as undergraduates and/or who perceive themselves as highly capable teachers may place less priority on classroom environment and/or may fail to develop skills in this area at the same rate as other teachers.

Our analyses also revealed that second-year teachers in schools with higher percentages of students eligible for free or reduced-price lunch received lower ratings for instructional scaffolding in ELA during year 2. This suggests that teachers in this sample struggled to improve their ELA skills in modeling, teaching conceptual and procedural strategy use, and providing feedback to students from impoverished families.

In mathematics, we reported that opportunities to learn strategies for teaching diverse students were associated with higher ratings for instructional scaffolding in mathematics. This suggests that foundational knowledge in how to teach students from diverse socioeconomic, racial/ethnic, and linguistic backgrounds can help second-year teachers strengthen their mathematics instructional skills in modeling, conceptual and procedural strategy use, and feedback.

Similar to ELA, we found that teaching in grades 3–5 as a second-year teacher was linked to higher PLATO mathematics scores in representations and organization of content. This finding, though, contrasts with our finding that first-year teachers in these grades had lower PLATO mathematics scores in representations and organization of content than first-year teachers in grades K–2. It may be that upper elementary mathematics content is harder to teach than lower elementary mathematics content. As a result, the upper elementary teachers in this sample seemed to strongly benefit from having an opportunity in their second year to teach the same demanding mathematics content a second time.

The finding that having relatively higher SAT/ACT scores was associated with higher disciplinary demand in mathematics suggests that high levels of general academic ability are helpful for second-year teachers' efforts to enact mathematics activities with high levels of cognitive demand and to engage students in extended discussions of their solutions to mathematical problems and their mathematical reasoning.

We found that Teachers of Color in this sample had higher ratings for instructional scaffolding in mathematics than white teachers and that male teachers had higher classroom environment scores than female teachers. We caution against reading too much into these findings, given the very small numbers of Teachers of Color ($N = 6$) and male teachers ($N = 4$) in the sample.

CONCLUSION

Overall, our three analyses provide insight into the complex nature of beginning teachers' development of ambitious instructional practices and the opportunities to learn associated with such development. While the novice teachers in our DAI study struggled to teach ambitiously in both ELA and mathematics, they did teach more ambitiously in their second year of teaching than in their first year, particularly in the disciplinary demand and representations and organization of content domains. In year 2, the beginning teachers engaged their students in ELA and mathematics tasks that included analysis, interpretation, and idea generation more often and communicated learning goals more clearly to their students than in year 1. They also improved in managing student behavior and time. The novices did not, however, demonstrate improvement in the instructional scaffolding domain, which includes modeling, teaching conceptual and procedural strategies, and providing feedback to make disciplinary concepts and practices accessible to students. These practices remained especially challenging for them.

We found a similarly complex relation between the opportunities to learn that novices reported encountering in their preparation programs and the ambitiousness of their teaching in years 1 and 2. Teacher candidates who reported more opportunities to learn about general principles and methods of instruction enacted more ambitious teaching practices in the disciplinary demand and instructional scaffolding domains in both ELA and mathematics as first-year teachers. In addition, teacher candidates who reported more opportunities to learn about, try out, and get feedback on enacting ambitious instructional strategies during student teaching employed more ambitious practices in the instructional scaffolding and representations and organizations of content domains in mathematics in their first year of teaching, while those who reported more opportunities to learn about strategies for teaching diverse learners managed student behavior and time in their classrooms more effectively during mathematics lessons. In year 2, only opportunities to learn about strategies for teaching diverse learners were associated with more ambitious instructional scaffolding practices in mathematics.

In ELA, we found that opportunities to learn about general principles and methods of instruction and strategies for teaching diverse learners, and opportunities to learn about, try out, and get feedback on enacting ambitious teaching strategies during student teaching were associated with second-year teachers employing more ambitious practices in the classroom environment and representations and organization of content domains. Overall, opportunities to learn about general principles and methods of instruction and strategies for teaching diverse learners, as well as opportunities to learn, try out, and get feedback enacting ambitious content-specific strategies during student teaching appear to be especially salient for beginning teachers and especially in relation to their mathematics instruction.

In the following chapter, we explore in more depth the complex and nuanced nature of beginning teachers' development of ambitious instructional practices through the cases of three novices who we followed from their preparation programs into their first three years of teaching. The cases examine how the beginning teachers make sense of and take up – or not- the opportunities to learn they encountered in their preparation programs in light of their professional goals and visions of teaching; their relationships with their students, colleagues, and school administrators; and the resources available in the schools and districts in which they begin their careers.

CHAPTER 4

Beginning Teachers' Development of Ambitious Instructional Practices

The Role of Teacher Preparation and School-Based Resources

Beginning teachers forge their instructional practices as they transition from being students in their preparation programs to becoming teachers of record responsible for the students in their classrooms and to the colleagues, administrators, families, and community members in their schools and districts. In chapter 3, we explored novice teachers' enactment of different ambitious instructional practices across their first two years of teaching and the opportunities to learn in their preparation programs that were associated with it. In this chapter, we examine in depth how three beginning elementary teachers developed their mathematics and English language arts (ELA) instruction as they interacted with students, colleagues, administrators, and others in the classrooms and schools where they began their careers. The three teachers—Jessica, Roberto, and Nora (all pseudonyms)—were among sixteen novices whom we followed from teacher preparation into their first three years of teaching as part of the Development of Ambitious Instruction (DAI) study. Though Jessica, Roberto, and Nora, like the other novices in the DAI study, struggled to teach ambitiously, their Protocol for Language Arts Teaching Observation (PLATO) scores in mathematics and ELA were among the more ambitious in the study. Their cases provide insight into how beginning elementary teachers can forge more ambitious teaching practices as they transition from teacher preparation into full-time teaching.

As we trace their development, we examine how Jessica, Roberto, and Nora selected and used the resources they encountered in their preparation programs and their schools and districts. Beginning teachers devote considerable time and effort to learning how to work with the resources available in their new schools and districts.[1] These resources include curriculum guides, textbooks, and instructional materials, such as mathematics manipulatives and worksheets, as well as the guidance and emotional support administrators and teaching colleagues might provide. Novice teachers also bring resources from their teacher preparation programs (TPPs), including practices for managing classrooms and teaching content and the frameworks and principles that undergird them.[2] In addition, as they forge their instructional practices, beginning teachers draw on the beliefs about teaching and learning that they form through their own experiences as learners in K–12 schools, preparation programs, and the schools they teach in.[3]

Though the availability of these varied resources is essential, whether the resources assist beginning teachers to teach more ambitiously depends on how the novices make sense of and utilize them. Their sensemaking is shaped, in turn, by the knowledge, beliefs, and emotions that beginning teachers bring from prior experiences and that they form as they engage in their work. Given their status as novices, their need to establish their competency as professionals further conditions whether and how they use resources. We use the term *personal sense* to capture this amalgam of cognitive, emotional, and motivational factors and how it shapes beginning teachers' resource use.[4]

In the sections that follow, we first categorize the different types of resources central to beginning teachers' development and describe how the concept of personal sense helps us understand novices' resource use. We then explore how Jessica, Roberto, and Nora each made sense of, selected, and used resources from their own experiences, their TPPs, and the schools and districts where they began their careers to construct their instructional practices in mathematics and ELA. Taken together, the cases reveal how opportunities to learn about and enact ambitious practices in teacher preparation can provide beginning teachers with conceptual and practical resources that can assist them in teaching more ambitiously as they also learn about and teach with school- and district-based resources. The cases further illustrate the complex role that social resources within schools and districts, especially guidance from colleagues and coaches, can play in novice teachers' instructional development. While these resources can support beginning teachers' efforts to teach more ambitiously, they can also run counter to them. Ultimately, the cases highlight how beginning teachers' sense of professional competence shapes whether and how they take up both teacher preparation- and school-based resources to cultivate more ambitious teaching practices.

RESOURCES AND BEGINNING TEACHER INSTRUCTIONAL DEVELOPMENT

Resources are central to beginning teachers' development of their instructional practices, including ambitious practices. Novices use them to guide and carry out their classroom practice. We distinguish among three types of resources: conceptual, practical, and social.[5]

Conceptual resources are the principles, frameworks, or visions of teaching and learning that teachers use to guide their instructional decisions. These include theories of learning, such as constructivist or behaviorist theories, and concepts, such as instructional scaffolding or backward design. Though they seldom articulated formal theories, the novices in our study described how concepts, such as student-centered teaching or a growth mindset, or frameworks, such as the workshop approach in ELA, influenced their decisions about managing their classrooms, planning lessons, or thinking about how to respond to student work. In addition to guiding their instructional decisions, conceptual resources also shape how beginning teachers imagine, think about, and assess their own teaching. In this way, they play a key role in novice teachers' construction of their teacher identities.

Practical resources, in contrast, are the concrete materials and the more specific classroom strategies and routines that teachers employ directly as they plan lessons or work with students. The practical resources made available by the schools and districts where novice teachers begin their careers, such as curriculum-pacing guides, textbooks and teachers' guides, sight word flashcards, and mathematics manipulatives, are especially influential.[6] Beginning teachers devote significant time and effort to learning how to teach with these resources. These materials support particular instructional routines and classroom practices, such as the number talks routine, during which teachers elicit students' personal problem-solving strategies to deepen their understanding of mathematical concepts and/or procedures, or guided reading groups, during which teachers work with small groups of students as they read leveled texts to build students' fluency, identify text features, and/or assist students in making inferences. Practical resources that facilitate students sharing and jointly examining their ideas play a critical role in ambitious instruction and its focus on deepening students' understanding of disciplinary concepts.

The support that administrators and colleagues provide beginning teachers also plays an important role in novices' instructional development. We view this support as a *social resource*. Social resources include emotional support that fosters beginning teachers' confidence and resiliency as it helps them deal productively with frustrations and challenges. They also include practical resources, like lesson plans or digital resources, that colleagues share with novice teachers. Colleagues can also offer guidance or advice and knowledge about different aspects of teaching, such as how to use curricular materials, how to respond to student learning, or how to address classroom management challenges. Guidance provides beginning teachers conceptual resources as it makes available ways of thinking about when, how, and why to use teaching approaches and/or their attendant practices.

As our cases in this chapter show both the availability and the interaction of these different types of resources shape beginning teachers' instructional development. Conceptual resources provide novices lenses through which to make sense of and utilize curricular and instructional materials to meet their students' needs. Without such frames, beginning teachers may use practical resources in ways that can limit their development of more ambitious instructional practices. Similarly, while the beginning teachers in our study typically found the practical resources their colleagues shared with them to be helpful in their day-to-day planning, it was the guidance from their colleagues and coaches, often in conjunction with conceptual resources from their teacher preparation programs, that helped them teach more ambitiously. The presence and combination of conceptual, practical, and social resources send powerful messages to novice teachers about the types of teaching and instructional practices valued by their school and district colleagues and administrators and contribute to their sense of their own professional competence as well as to their instructional practice.

BEGINNING TEACHERS' PERSONAL SENSE AND RESOURCE USE

While the nature and availability of the resources described in the foregoing section influence beginning teachers' development of their instruction, how novices make sense of and use available resources ultimately determines whether and how the resources help them teach ambitiously.[7] How beginning teachers select, modify, and create resources, in turn, depends on numerous factors, including their knowledge and beliefs about teaching and learning, school and district mandates, and their relationships and interactions with their colleagues and students. Novice teachers' resource use is further conditioned by the teachers' desire to establish their professional competence and by the emotions they experience as they navigate the myriad demands and challenges of teaching.

We use the term *personal sense* to capture this nexus of influences and how it shapes teachers' perceptions and use of resources. Drawn from sociocultural theories of learning,[8] our conception of personal sense encompasses the meanings that beginning teachers make of their work as teachers and the significance they apply to that work. As they interact with their students, colleagues, and others, novice teachers receive messages about the types of teachers people in their school contexts see as competent and about the types of instructional practices that are effective with their students and valued by their school and district colleagues. They also take in messages about the resources available to them, including those from teacher preparation and their own schooling experiences, and whether and how they should use the resources in their teaching. Beginning teachers interpret these messages, or develop their personal sense of them, through the knowledge, beliefs, motivations, and emotions that they have built up or experienced over time, including and especially as K–12 students and preservice teacher candidates.

Novice teachers who hold personal theories of teaching and learning aligned with ambitious instruction, for example, are more likely to use curricular materials that engage students in exploring multiple strategies for solving mathematical problems than those who do not hold these theories. If, however, their school colleagues and administrators value teaching discrete mathematics skills and preferred strategies, novices might feel compelled to follow suit, especially if their own challenges learning mathematics as students raise self-doubts about their abilities to teach mathematics effectively. Other beginning teachers—especially those with more positive experiences learning mathematics and who encountered ambitious conceptual and practical resources in their TPPs—might find ways to prioritize their use of these resources.

Beginning teachers' personal sense evolves as it both shapes and is shaped by their early-career experiences. As they transition from being students to being full-time teachers, novices encounter the full range and weight of teachers' professional demands and responsibilities for the first time. This often creates tensions between beginning teachers' past and present beliefs about teaching and learning; the practices they want to, can, and feel they should enact; and how they view themselves and their professional goals. Novice teachers can experience these tensions as opportunities for learning or, if the experiences generate negative emotions, as impediments to it. As such, these tensions can enable or inhibit their development of ambitious instruction.

THREE CASES OF BEGINNING TEACHERS' RESOURCE USE AND DEVELOPMENT OF MORE AMBITIOUS INSTRUCTION

We turn now to explore how Jessica, Roberto, and Nora developed their instructional practice in both ELA and mathematics as they made sense of and utilized the different resources available to them. As Table 4.1 shows, Jessica and Roberto graduated from Cardinal's TPP, while Nora graduated from Meadowlark's TPP. The schools where Roberto and Nora taught served higher percentages of Students of Color and students living in poverty, as indicated by the percentage of students eligible for federal free and reduced-price lunches, than the schools where Jessica taught. Further, while Roberto and Nora remained in the same schools from year 1 to year 3, Jessica moved to a different school between year 1 and year 2. Jessica taught third grade

TABLE 4.1 Focal teacher information and school contexts

Beginning teacher	*Gender & racial identities*	*Teacher preparation program*	*Grade level taught*	*School demographics*
Jessica	Female, white	Cardinal	3rd	Year 1 school White 67% African American 2% Latinx 6% Native American 1% Asian 22% Multiracial 4% FRL⁺ 22% Years 2 & 3 school White 88% African American 3% Latinx 6% Asian 2% Multiracial 2% FRL⁺ 9%
Roberto	Male, Latinx	Cardinal	4th	White 25% African American 7% Latinx 58% Native American 1% Asian 6% Multiracial 4% FRL⁺ 87%
Nora	Female, white	Meadowlark	1st Y1; 2nd Y2 &Y3	White 49% African American 19% Latinx 21% Asian 6% Multiracial 5% FRL⁺ 55%

Note: ⁺FRL = The percentage of students within a school eligible to receive federally funded free or reduced-price lunch is an indicator of the concentration of low-income students in a school.

and Roberto taught fourth grade all three years. Nora moved from teaching first grade in year 1 to second grade in years 2 and 3.

Figures 4.1 and 4.2 compare Jessica's, Roberto's, and Nora's PLATO composite scores in mathematics and ELA from year 1 to year 3 with the mean composite scores of the sixteen case study teacher sample.

FIGURE 4.1 Jessica's, Roberto's, and Nora's PLATO ELA scores, by year

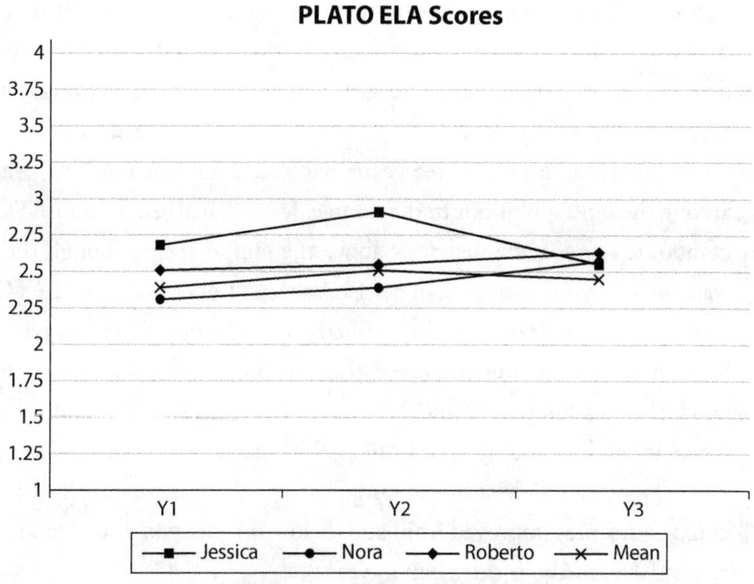

FIGURE 4.2 Jessica's, Roberto's, and Nora's PLATO mathematics scores, by year

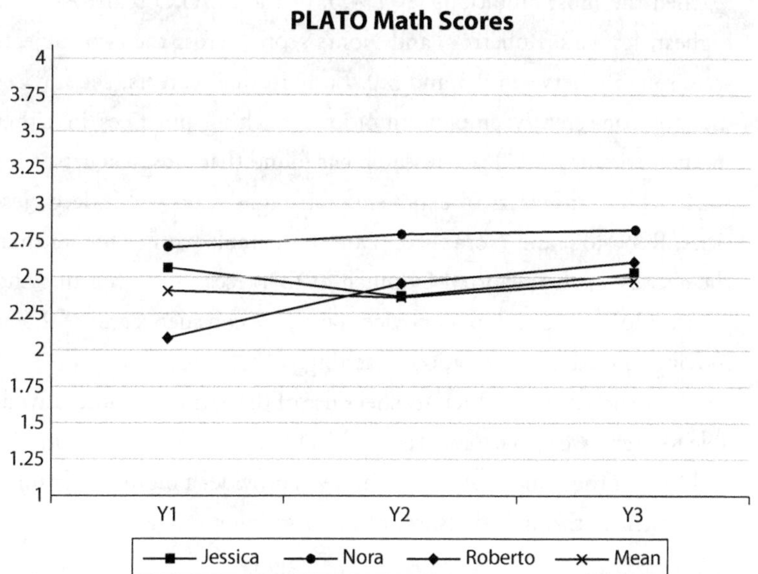

PLATO scores range from 1.0 to 4.0, with 1.0 indicating that, on average, there is no evidence of ambitious instruction across the PLATO domains, 2.0 indicating there is limited evidence, 3.0 indicating evidence with some weakness, and 4.0 indicating consistent strong evidence. Jessica's ELA PLATO composite scores remained above the sample mean across the three years; her year 2 ELA score (2.91) was among the most ambitious in the sample. Jessica's mathematics PLATO composite scores remained at or above the sample mean, though they were, on the whole, lower than her ELA scores. Roberto's ELA PLATO composite scores started and remained above the sample mean, while his mathematics scores improved from below the mean in year 1 to above the mean in years 2 and 3. Conversely, Nora's PLATO composite scores in mathematics ranged from 2.79 in year 1 to 2.82 in year 2 and were among the highest in the sample across all three years. Her ELA composite scores improved from at or below the mean in years 1 and 2, respectively, to above the mean in year 3.

As indicated, none of the three novices' PLATO composite scores reached the most ambitious level, 4.0, of the PLATO scale. At their highest, Jessica's, Roberto's, and Nora's scores across the two subjects were roughly between 2.5 and 3.0. Early in their careers, the novices did not consistently employ ambitious teaching practices in either mathematics or ELA. Prior research has found that most teachers, even those with many years of experience, struggle to do so.[9] Indeed, Jessica's, Roberto's, and Nora's scores are comparable with or higher than the average scores reported by much of this research. Given this and Jessica, Roberto, and Nora's novice status, we consider scores of 2.5 as moving toward more ambitious teaching.

As we describe here each teacher's use of the various resources available to them, we also explore their PLATO scores in both mathematics and ELA at the dimension level. This level provides a more fine-grained assessment of the ambitiousness of the beginning teachers' instruction as it relates to more specific types of practices. Given that Jessica's, Roberto's, and Nora's scores mostly clustered within a narrow range, we consider the novices' resource use in light of the pattern of their scores across the dimensions and subjects.

Jessica

Jessica began her career as a long-term substitute teacher in a school located near Cardinal University, where she had completed her TPP, and the school district she had attended as a K–12 student. In year 2, Jessica took a full-time teaching position in a different nearby district, remaining there through year 3. The two schools enrolled similar student populations, though the second school, similar to the ones she had attended, enrolled a higher percentage of white students and a lower percentage of students living in poverty.

Jessica consistently described her transition from pre- to in-service teaching and between her first and second schools as "very smooth." She viewed her own beliefs about teaching and learning and those she encountered at Cardinal's TPP and in the schools where she taught as highly aligned. Both districts where Jessica began her career had adopted the same ELA and mathematics curricula, furthering her sense of continuity. From year 1, she felt well prepared to teach both subjects. At the same time, she encountered and made use of more social resources in her schools to develop her ELA instruction than her mathematics instruction.

ELA: Continuity and coherent support In both schools where Jessica taught, she centered the development of her ELA instruction on the district ELA curriculum.[10] Both schools' districts had recently adopted the same ELA program, which emphasized a workshop model focused on engaging students in reading and writing authentic texts and teaching reading and writing skills through mini-lessons, individual and small-group work, and whole-class debriefings.

Although she focused on teaching the curriculum, Jessica drew on practical and conceptual resources from Cardinal's TPP to do so. She viewed the district curricula as closely aligned with the approach and practices she encountered in Cardinal's ELA methods courses. Those courses taught candidates the principles and practices of a workshop model, though not the specific version that Jessica's districts had adopted. The courses also exposed candidates to methods for teaching and assessing ELA skills, including phonics, word identification, fluency, vocabulary, and comprehension, and for supporting diverse learners. Jessica reported using instructional routines she learned at Cardinal, including "how you model and . . . use mentor texts . . . the independent practice and then the share," and enacting them in the workshop model that guided her "everyday teaching." She thus took both conceptual and practical resources from Cardinal's TPP to guide and enact her ELA instruction while she focused on learning how to teach the district curricula.

In year 1, Jessica described her preparation as an "advantage" that contributed to her confidence in teaching ELA: "I have a bit of an advantage as a first-year teacher. This is what I was taught for the last three years. I feel like some of this is brand new for . . . veteran older teachers . . . but for me as a new teacher . . . I was just taught (this) in college."

Jessica's preparation enabled her to form reciprocal relationships with her colleagues, including her veteran colleagues. In year 1, she used "a lot" of her veteran grade-level teammates' "strategies and input." Yet, she also noted that because the "reader's workshop [was] new for her [teammate], she's saying that she is learning from me." The alignment of TPP conceptual and practical resources with district-based ELA practical resources enabled Jessica to establish her professional competence among her colleagues from year 1.

In years 2 and 3, Jessica continued to feel that Cardinal's TPP had provided her with a strong foundation to teach ELA. At the same time, she deepened her understanding of the workshop model and its practices through the coherent support she received in her school. This included professional development the district had purchased with the ELA program. Teachers met several times during the school year with program coaches. In year 2, Jessica reported that these resources "really help(ed)" her "grow as a new teacher" by identifying a focus for her learning, specifically, how to more effectively use small-group instruction to provide students with additional ELA practice. In year 3, she further highlighted her growth in the program's mini-lessons and active engagement components. She attributed this growth to information she garnered from the program's teacher's guide and guidance from program coaches.

In years 2 and 3, Jessica's colleagues also contributed to the development of her ELA instruction. They shared lesson plans and provided guidance as they reviewed student assessment data and planned together. Her description of a unit on main ideas illustrates how she used these social resources in conjunction with the district's ELA curriculum:

> Most of the time I followed the lessons in [the teachers' guide] and there's an online component that I really like. . . . We're currently ending a data team cycle as a third-grade team on main idea and supporting details . . . a lot of students were still doing the topic rather than the main idea, or the details did not match up. . . . Some students still haven't mastered that. So, we're going to pull a small group and do a mini-lessons on that. [My grade-level colleague] has a lot of mini-lessons and resources that I'm going to take from her and use as well.

In teaching the unit, Jessica continued to follow the district-mandated ELA curriculum and utilized its practical resources. She also used resources from her data team colleagues as they jointly determined how they would support students who struggled with key unit reading skills and shared lesson plans with her. In this way, the sharing and guidance her colleagues provided Jessica directly aligned with the practical resources in the district curriculum.

By year 3, Jessica articulated a commitment to the district's ELA curriculum and its pedagogical approach.

> I love the active engagement pieces. The turn-and-talk. . . . I was shy growing up. So just having students talk out their thoughts and ideas without having to share out to everyone, I like that structure. Making a chart sometimes will help for that, too. Then they really get to try it out on their own in that mini-lessons time frame. Then the basic reader's workshop of them moving on to independent time after was really something done in college. That share time at the end again gives them time to talk about the book they read with partners. They love to share that with me, too.

Jessica described the workshop framework and its attendant routines with highly positive emotional language, drawing personal connections to it. She "love[d]" the active engagement activities and "like[d]" the turn-and-talk routine, which supported the learning of students who were shy, as she had been. That same year, she started to use a workshop "style," which she described as moving "from whole-class to guided practice and gradual release to independent work," in her mathematics teaching as well, further signaling her commitment to the approach.

As Jessica attended to her students' learning, through both her data team and monitoring her students' reading and writing in her classroom, she did exert more discretion in how she taught the district's ELA curriculum. In year 3, she described modifying the ELA curriculum: "Basically, when I go in and follow these lessons, I think about what students are going to get out of them. I make sure it will benefit my students first. Then I'll either keep the connection or modify the connection in the teacher guide. I'll clarify the learning target." Thus, while she continued to "follow" the district's ELA curriculum, Jessica adapted lessons and clarified learning goals to support her students' development as readers and writers.

Mathematics: Continuity with few social resources Jessica also perceived an alignment among the resources available to forge her mathematics instruction. These resources included conceptual resources drawn from her own experiences as a mathematics learner. Jessica frequently described how much she had enjoyed learning mathematics as a K–12 and university student. For her, math was "a subject that I'm not only strong in, but just love." As a teacher, she wanted to "pass on" her "passion" for the subject to her students, which she attributed to her "growth mind set." She wanted to instill this mind set in her students. In year 1, she asserted, "I don't want to hear any student in my classroom ever say, 'I'm no good at math,' or 'Math isn't for me,' because math can be a part of everyone's lives."

Jessica believed that Cardinal's TPP courses and the mathematics curriculum adopted by both districts she taught in endorsed a similar growth mind set. This alignment was central to the development of her mathematics instruction:

> I'd always had that mind set, but I never really realized how much you have to make it explicit in your classroom in order to make it shine. [The mathematics methods professor] woke certain kids up that were the ones that did not want to be there and really got them going. And then there were different research articles that we would read about having the growth mind set and the eight mathematical practices and making sure that students explain their thinking more often and it's not just rote multiplication and memorization. All through the course I was, "That makes sense." It reinforced, but it also put words to what I was thinking. And then here too, using this [district-adopted math program]. A lot of math programs I saw throughout student teaching or the placement clinics, I would just take certain parts of to make my own, but this I follow more because it has a lot more of my mind set.

The Cardinal mathematics methods course provided Jessica conceptual and practical resources that enabled her to articulate her beliefs about teaching and learning mathematics and the instructional strategies, such as eliciting students' mathematical thinking, to enact them as a teacher. The mathematics curriculum in the districts she taught in further provided conceptual and practical resources that she "followed" because they were aligned with her beliefs and the vision of mathematics teaching that she encountered in Cardinal's TPP.

As in ELA, in mathematics in years 2 and 3, Jessica focused her mathematics instruction on teaching the district's curriculum. Unlike in ELA, however, she did much of this work alone and in her own classroom. She did seek and receive guidance from a grade-level colleague when she felt a lesson did not go well. She also attended a conference with the district's mathematics coach on the recommendation of a school administrator, who viewed Jessica as a highly competent mathematics teacher. She did not, however, articulate what she learned from these resources or how she used them in her teaching, as she did with the ELA professional development. She constructed her mathematics teaching primarily through her own reading, interpretation, and use of the district curriculum, all of which were framed by her own beliefs about teaching and learning mathematics and the conceptual and practical resources from Cardinal's TPP.

The district mathematics curriculum offered teachers a plethora of practical resources. These included a teacher's guide for the mathematics program, purchased by the district, that provided highly detailed lesson plans, which Jessica described as "scripted." The curriculum focused on the use of visual models and opportunities for students to develop and share problem-solving strategies and included daily routines designed to support students' pattern-finding, as well as games to support their development of computational fluency. Jessica described the program as "do[ing] a good job with that more rigorous thinking and explaining your thinking, understanding where that came from." She also felt that the program encouraged a growth mind set.

As Jessica taught the curriculum, she observed how the lessons sparked students' interest and engagement by encouraging them to share their mathematical reasoning. She described a lesson she taught using the curriculum:

> It gives [students] access to all of the strategies that we have been working on throughout the unit. We do the same thing during the unit on addition and subtraction. We create the same chart, and it gives ownership to the ways of thinking and strategies by using their names. They are like, "Ooh, this is Bobby's way." And that's taken from [the mathematics program]. I just love the enthusiasm for them wanting to share. . . . Some strategies that I wouldn't have thought of originally come up usually and it's just like a fun lesson because if I'm thinking, "Oh wow, I didn't think of that." The third graders are definitely thinking that too as they are listening to their peers.

For Jessica, the district mathematics curriculum fostered students' ownership of and enjoyment in their learning as it encouraged them to articulate their mathematics reasoning. In this way, it assisted her in sharing her passion for mathematics with her students.

Over time, Jessica asserted some discretion in using the mathematics curriculum, driven largely by what she felt would best support her students' learning.

> I always take that lesson and curriculum map and read it over and see if I want to strictly follow the lesson or add in something. Today I added in the exit slip. It's actually a page taken from the [curriculum] materials, but it wasn't stated in the lesson to do that. I wanted to have that formative assessment. I like exit slips or different formative assessments so that I always know where my kids are at and where I want to take them next. It's a good gauge of how the lesson went overall. Like do I need to revisit some of the items or did most of my class get it and I just need to pull a small group?

In years 2 and 3, Jessica determined how strictly she would follow the district mathematics curriculum. In the foregoing comment, she describes how she modified the curriculum by adding an exit slip, a practical resource she took from her Cardinal mathematics methods course, to assess the effectiveness of her lessons and determine future plans. In another case, rather than using an activity laid out in the curriculum, she created a whole-class activity to structure students' use of mathematics manipulatives and maintain their focus on learning. Jessica had originally learned how to teach with manipulatives in her methods course. Her principal also provided some guidance on how to manage students' use of manipulatives. By year 3, Jessica had established a set of teaching practices in mathematics that integrated resources from her own experiences, Cardinal's TPP, and the schools and districts where she taught. She did not have access, however, to the coherent set of social resources that she found so powerful in ELA to help her develop her mathematics instruction.

Jessica's PLATO scores Table 4.2 reports Jessica's PLATO scores in ELA and mathematics for each dimension each year. As noted earlier, given the novice status of teachers, such as Jessica, who participated in the DAI study and the persistent research finding that experienced teachers find teaching ambitiously as measured by PLATO difficult, we consider PLATO dimension scores of 2.5 or higher as moving toward more ambitious teaching. We bolded those scores accordingly.

In both subjects, Jessica's classroom environment scores indicate that she consistently managed student behavior and class time in ways that facilitated student learning. In ELA, some of her highest scores in the instructional domains were in the intellectual challenge and text-based instruction dimensions. She was developing her skills engaging students in reading and writing tasks that involved interpreting and/or producing authentic texts. Her scores in the purpose dimension were also among her highest, reaching a 3.56 on PLATO's four-point scale. In years 2 and 3, Jessica more consistently communicated learning goals to her students and how the lessons she assigned her students supported their development as readers and writers. Finally, though her scores in the instructional scaffolding domain were on the whole low, she did

TABLE 4.2 Jessica's PLATO ELA and mathematics scores, by dimension and year

PLATO domain: dimension	*ELA Y1*	*ELA Y2*	*ELA Y3*	*Math Y1*	*Math Y2*	*Math Y3*
Instructional scaffolding: modeling	1.50	1.94	1.63	2.25	1.75	1.92
Instructional scaffolding: conceptual strategy use and instruction	1.67	2.06	**2.63**	1.42	1.75	2.42
Instructional scaffolding: procedural strategy use and instruction	1.08	1.11	1.75	1.50	1.92	2.00
Instructional scaffolding: feedback	2.08	**2.67**	2.38	2.25	2.08	2.33
Disciplinary demand: intellectual challenge	**3.08**	**2.78**	**2.63**	2.25	2.42	**2.67**
Disciplinary demand: classroom discourse	2.25	2.17	1.50	**2.75**	2.08	2.08
Disciplinary demand text-based instruction	**3.08**	**2.78**	**2.63**	X	X	X
Representations/organization of content: representation of content	**2.58**	**2.64**	1.50	**2.58**	1.83	1.58
Representations/organization of content: purpose	2.33	**3.56**	**3.00**	2.00	2.00	2.33
Classroom environment: behavior management	**3.92**	**4.00**	**3.75**	**3.92**	**3.67**	**3.33**
Classroom environment: time management	**3.67**	**3.72**	**3.25**	**3.25**	**3.17**	**3.83**

Note: We consider PLATO dimension scores of 2.5 or higher as moving toward more ambitious teaching. We bolded those scores accordingly.

build some skill teaching conceptual instructional strategies and providing students substantive feedback to improve their ELA skills.

In mathematics, Jessica's scores in the instructional dimensions seldom reached 2.5 on PLATO's four-point scale. One of her highest scores was in the intellectual challenge dimension, suggesting that she had developed some skill engaging her students in a mix of learning tasks that, while often rote, did include problem-solving and analysis. Her other highest scores were in the classroom discourse and representations of content dimensions, but only in year 1; her year 2 and year 3 scores were low in both dimensions. Jessica's scores in the conceptual and procedural strategy dimensions also showed some improvement, though they remained in the 1's and lower 2's.

Overall, Jessica's PLATO scores suggest that as she learned to use the ELA and mathematics curricula, she built her skills teaching activities that included components of interpretation and analysis in both subjects. Her scores on the whole, however, were higher in ELA than in mathematics. The pattern of the scores across the subjects points to the role that school-based social resources can play in supporting beginning teachers' development of more ambitious teaching practices. Jessica perceived a strong alignment between the conceptual and practical resources she drew from Cardinal's TPP and the resources available in the districts' mathematics and ELA curricula. She further expressed a passion for teaching mathematics and perceived a close alignment with the conceptual resources she garnered from her own mathematics learning experiences. She did not have access, however, to the type of coherent guidance from coaches and colleagues that she had in ELA. Whereas she utilized this guidance to teach ELA, she largely developed her mathematics teaching on her own as she implemented the district mathematics curriculum in her classroom. Her PLATO scores across the subjects suggest that she needed more support in using the mathematics curriculum to teach more ambitiously.

Roberto

Roberto, also a graduate of Cardinal's TPP, chose to teach in the district he had attended as a K–12 student and where some of his family members were students and educators. As Table 4.1 shows, the school he taught in served a racially and ethnically diverse student body. A large number of students, 65 percent, were Latino, and most, 87 percent, were classified as low income. In year 1, Roberto explained his reason for teaching in the district: "This is my city. I was born and raised here. I am putting my heart and soul into this because this is where my eight-year-old sister goes." For Roberto, teaching in the district was emotional and moral work grounded in familial and community relationships.

In contrast to most beginning teachers in our study, who identified as white females and seldom discussed how their gender or racial identities shaped their teaching, Roberto viewed his gender and racial identities, along with his community ties, as resources for establishing his competence as a teacher. From year 1, school administrators and colleagues praised his strong classroom management skills and positive student relationships. While he appreciated the praise, Roberto felt that by attributing his success to his being a Man of Color in a field dominated by white females, his mostly white female colleagues negated the hard work and skill he devoted to building warm, productive relationships with his students. He believed that being from the community and Puerto Rican, like many of his students, helped him manage his classroom, as he avoided the "cultural dissonance" that other teachers experienced. But he also attributed his strong classroom management to his competence, noting, "My deck of cards is stacked, but I'm playing them right."

Roberto's positive relationships with his students reflected his commitment to their learning. He described his students as "hard workers. They have grit. They're eager to learn and they can perform at a high level." He contrasted this view with a deficit view he felt many of his colleagues held: "Some people say, 'We are a high priority district, 80 percent free and reduced lunch. We need to give these kids charity.' No! Because I was one of these kids and I made my way to Cardinal University. So, I have very high expectations for them. . . . I was one of them." Although it created some tensions with his colleagues, Roberto maintained a steadfast belief in his students' capabilities and a personal commitment to their learning.

Roberto's commitment to his students' learning shaped his instructional practices in both ELA and mathematics. He frequently described himself as a "student-centered teacher." This identity informed his instructional development in both subjects and how he utilized the resources available to him.

ELA: Increased confidence and commitment to the district curriculum Like Jessica, Roberto focused much of his efforts on learning to teach the district's ELA curriculum. Unlike Jessica, he did not report drawing on specific conceptual or practical resources from Cardinal ELA methods courses. While Roberto believed the principles and practices promoted in these courses broadly aligned with the district ELA curriculum, he viewed them as providing "a foundation" for his teaching rather than identifying specific practices or approaches that he used in or that guided his planning and instruction. Instead, he focused his daily planning and teaching on the practical resources associated with the district's ELA curriculum. The curriculum included a detailed pacing guide that delineated weekly units with learning objectives, themes, focal concepts and skills, anchor texts, and writing prompts. It also specified instructional strategies and formats that included whole-class skills lessons; whole-class close readings of anchor texts using a set of "Good Reader" questions; guided reading groups with leveled texts; and independent reading and writing time supported by a digital reading program. Writing instruction centered on students constructing evidence-based arguments in response to prompts typically related to an anchor text and using a restate-answer-cite–explain-summarize formula.

Roberto closely followed the district curriculum, using its practical resources, such as writing prompts and anchor texts, and enacting the specified instructional routines, like guided reading groups. Having "everything laid out . . . alleviate(d) the stress" he associated with being a novice teacher; he did not have to "search in the dark" to find and assemble materials. Despite this, in the first half of year 1, Roberto found teaching reading challenging. He felt especially unsure of how best to facilitate guided reading groups even though he thought the instructional routine aligned with the workshop model he encountered in his Cardinal ELA methods courses. Early in year 1, he described teaching reading as "just so much." He felt that his own struggles with reading as an elementary student further contributed to his lack of confidence in his ELA teaching.

In years 1 and 2, Roberto received little guidance regarding his ELA instruction. Because the district curriculum was so prescriptive, his grade-level colleagues shared resources with him, but they did not plan lessons together. Their conversations about their ELA teaching did not go much further than exchanging materials to augment the curriculum. Because half of his grade-level teammates were either early-career teachers or new to the school, Roberto felt they could offer minimal guidance. Further, because the reading coach had teaching duties, he did not receive the guidance he wanted from her; the reading coach was not able to work with him in his classroom, observe and give him feedback on his teaching, or model instructional strategies.

By the middle of year 1, after becoming more familiar with the curriculum, Roberto expressed more confidence and enjoyment in teaching ELA. He came to "love" the ELA curriculum. He attributed this change to his students' growth in reading and writing. The district's teacher evaluation system tracked each teacher's students' standardized test scores in ELA and mathematics. As part of Roberto's year 1 evaluation, the school's vice principal praised him for his students' growth in their ELA scores. He also observed his students' positive engagement with the assigned texts and activities. By the end of year 1, he reflected on his ELA teaching, saying, "I think we've grown together. I've grown as a teacher. . . . I've seen the kids make tremendous growth." He tied his growth as an ELA teacher directly to his students' growth as readers and writers, evoking his identity as a student-centered teacher.

Roberto's enthusiasm for teaching ELA and the district's curriculum continued into years 2 and 3. He felt better able to facilitate discussions about texts that responded to his students' interests. In year 2, he engaged students in discussions of the issues the texts addressed, many of which he viewed as quite weighty: "I love the close reads. They're very heavy. Even [with] Lou Gehrig. He had ALS and he died. That's heavy. And even, you know, we just talked about Japanese internment camps and the kids were like, 'Does this happen anymore?' And I said, 'What do you think?' and then we talked about the phobia of Japanese Americans and a kid related it to the phobia of immigrants and I took it a step further and related it to the phobia of Muslims. So, it's very in-depth."

As he taught the assigned texts, over time, Roberto engaged students more substantively with them, helping students to build their understanding of themes and draw connections with the world beyond the texts. He continued to report in year 3 that he "loved" ELA and that "the kids do, too. They love to ask questions and connect the dots about reading and writing," connecting his growth in teaching ELA, again, to his students' learning.

By year 3, Roberto asserted some discretion in what and how he taught ELA. He selected books and materials from the curriculum and for guided reading groups that he believed "work[ed] well for [him] and the kids." He continued to describe himself, however, as a "real follower" of the curriculum both because of the vulnerability he associated with being an untenured novice and because he believed the curriculum fostered his students' learning. This included the guided reading program the district adopted in year 3. Roberto "liked" the new program because it provided teachers a "shared language" to use with their students. Most importantly, the new reading coach came into his classroom to model how to facilitate guided reading groups, cofacilitated groups with him, and provided him feedback on his facilitation. He viewed the reading coach as a "wealth of knowledge." She especially helped him work with students who struggled with comprehension while he continued to maintain high expectations for their learning.

The coach's guidance aligned with his positive view of his students' capacities and deepened his attention to their learning.

Mathematics: Increased coherence amid collegial tensions Roberto similarly centered the development of his mathematics instruction on the district's mathematics curriculum, which contained a scope-and-sequence pacing guide as well as pre- and postassessments and what he referred to as "a lot of materials." Unlike in ELA, in mathematics the district allowed teachers to "decide how to teach it all." In year 1, the district adopted a mathematics textbook with digital resources centered on the mathematical practices delineated in the Common Core State Standards and differentiated resources to provide students support or enrichment opportunities. That year, the district also required teachers to devote twenty minutes each day during their mathematics block for students to work individually on a digital program aimed at building their conceptual understanding through puzzles and problem-solving. In year 2, the district allowed teachers to schedule students' daily use of the program. Roberto moved the twenty-minute block to the end of the school day to allow for more instructional time during his math block.

Unlike many of his colleagues, Roberto was enthusiastic about the district's mathematics curriculum. The curriculum aligned with his own beliefs about teaching and learning, conceptual and practical resources from Cardinal's TPP courses, and school-based guidance. The curriculum's focus on differentiation aligned with Roberto's student-centered teacher identity. Its emphasis on exploring multiple problem-solving strategies further aligned with the focus on eliciting and expanding students' mathematical reasoning and exploring multiple representations that he encountered in Cardinal's TPP mathematics methods course and the mathematics course for elementary teachers that Roberto referenced in our interviews with him. In addition, the district-appointed mathematics coach provided guidance that supported this vision and built his confidence in teaching mathematics.

During years 1 and 2, Roberto reported that the mathematics coach "pushed [me] to do better" by working with him in his classroom and modeling how to use curricular materials to differentiate instruction and elicit students' thinking.

In year 2, Roberto's work with his teaching colleagues also contributed to his mathematics instruction. That year, the principal appointed him the grade-level team leader. Although, given his novice status, this created some tension with his colleagues, he committed to following the district curriculum and led the team in jointly examining assessment data to identify students for biweekly mathematics intervention support. The district mathematics coach assisted the team with this work, both in team meetings and in teachers' classrooms.

Examining student assessment data and working with the mathematics coach contributed to Roberto's increased attention to his students' mathematics learning. Throughout year 2 and year 3 interviews, he described several instances in which he identified and addressed skills and content that his students struggled with as he led whole-class activities or as he monitored students' work on independent learning tasks. For example, during a year 2 lesson, as students completed independent work, Roberto realized they were "struggling to conceptualize a gram." In response, he "pulled out the visuals" and led the class in comparing the amounts of water in an eyedropper, a jug, and the class fishtank. During a whole-class lesson in year 3, Roberto encouraged students to use different grouping strategies, including those they generated themselves, to solve division problems. After the lesson, he explained, "I'm trying to get them to see there's a million different ways to solve a problem. You choose the way that works in your brain." He also felt that by year 3, he had gained a "deeper understanding" of differentiation from working with his students. He realized that he needed to provide students more "scaffolding" rather than simply having them complete the "reteach" or "enrich" work sheets in the district's math program.

Roberto also found some of the practical resources and guidance that his colleagues shared helpful to his growth as a mathematics teacher, though he experienced some tensions with his colleagues. On the one hand, during year 1, he and his grade-level colleagues planned together. For example, after the team discussed their challenges in teaching factors, one of his colleagues found a strategy online focused on factor rainbows. Roberto subsequently used the strategy in years 2 and 3. On the other hand, he rejected his colleagues' resistance to the district mathematics curriculum. In year 3, he reported that his colleagues "push[ed] back against" the curriculum's emphasis on multiple algorithms. He disagreed, noting, "Kids like the lattice method and the partial products methods. For me, half the battle is fought because I am young and I did just learn all of these strategies. So it definitely aligns with what I think." The emphasis on multiple algorithms aligned not only with his own views about teaching and learning mathematics but also with conceptual and practical resources from Cardinal's TPP. In contrast to his more veteran colleagues, he felt well prepared by his TPP experiences to use the practical and conceptual resources in the district's mathematics curriculum. In this case, he perceived his novice status as an advantage.

Notably, in year 3, Roberto devoted less time to developing his mathematics teaching. The district increased its focus on raising ELA test scores in response to state policy pressures and budget constraints that reduced the support mathematics coaches could provide to teachers. In response, he began to reject some of the mathematics coach's guidance, such as creating a math word wall to build students' mathematical vocabulary, as "unrealistic," noting, "Who has time for that. . . . They just gave us a new writing curriculum [a week before]. . . . So be realistic. Sometimes you just have to shut your door and teach." Roberto also felt "frustrated" by his principal's demands that teachers devote even breakfast time with students to teaching reading. He felt that other subjects, including mathematics, were being overlooked. This ran counter to his belief "in the well-rounded child." While he continued to "love" the district mathematics curriculum and felt increasingly confident in his mathematics teaching, he felt "pressure," especially as an untenured teacher, to "compromise" to comply with testing mandates.

Roberto's PLATO scores Table 4.3 reports Roberto's scores in ELA and mathematics for years 1 through 3 across the eleven PLATO dimensions. Though his scores were somewhat lower in the time management dimension in mathematics, largely attributable to the challenges of managing differentiated activities, the classroom environment scores indicate that Roberto managed student behavior and instructional time in ways that consistently facilitated his students' learning.

TABLE 4.3 Roberto's PLATO ELA and mathematics scores by dimension and year

PLATO domain: dimension	*ELA Y1*	*ELA Y2*	*ELA Y3*	*Math Y1*	*Math Y2*	*Math Y3*
Instructional scaffolding: modeling	1.42	1.25	2.1	2.25	1.92	2.44
Instructional scaffolding: conceptual strategy use and instruction	1.50	1.58	1.42	1.25	1.58	2.31
Instructional scaffolding: procedural strategy use and instruction	1.52	1.50	1.69	2.08	2.42	**2.81**
Instructional scaffolding: feedback	**2.50**	**2.50**	2.44	**2.50**	2.25	2.47
Disciplinary demand: intellectual challenge	2.00	2.36	**2.72**	1.58	2.42	2.17
Disciplinary demand: classroom discourse	2.52	2.39	1.78	1.50	1.94	1.97
Disciplinary demand text-based instruction	2.00	2.36	**2.72**	X	X	X
Representations/organization of content: representation of content	**2.62**	**2.83**	2.44	1.83	2.33	2.47
Representations of content: purpose	2.17	2.33	2.17	2.17	2.00	**2.67**
Classroom environment: behavior management	**3.80**	**3.31**	**4.00**	**3.08**	**3.67**	**3.69**
Classroom environment: time management	**3.15**	**3.36**	**3.53**	2.42	**3.17**	**2.83**

Note: We consider PLATO dimension scores of 2.5 or higher as moving toward more ambitious teaching. We bolded those scores accordingly.

In ELA, some of Roberto's highest scores were in the intellectual demand and text-based instruction dimensions. His scores in these dimensions also improved each year. His year 1 and year 2 ELA scores in the feedback and representation of content dimensions were also among his highest. Roberto's ELA PLATO scores remained low in the purpose dimension and in the remaining dimensions of instructional scaffolding.

Roberto developed his ELA instruction largely through utilizing the practical resources provided by the district's prescriptive ELA curriculum. His PLATO scores suggest that he built some skill engaging students in more demanding intellectual tasks as he learned to teach with this curriculum. For at least his first two years, however, he had few social resources available to support the development of his ELA instruction. Further, Roberto seldom drew on ELA-specific conceptual or practical resources from Cardinal's TPP, drawing instead on a more generic concept of "student-centered teaching." His PLATO scores suggest that he needed further support to develop more ambitious practices in most instructional dimensions.

Roberto employed a wider array of resources to develop his mathematics instruction than he did to develop his ELA instruction. In addition to the practical resources colleagues shared with him, he received guidance from the district mathematics coach and drew on conceptual resources from Cardinal's TPP as he enacted the district mathematics curriculum. Though most of his PLATO scores across the different dimensions remained low, they suggest that these resources assisted him in building some skills in more clearly articulating purpose, or the learning goals of the mathematics tasks he assigned his students, and in teaching procedural strategies more explicitly. Notably, his scores in most of the instructional scaffolding dimensions, though low, were on the whole higher than his ELA scores in instructional scaffolding. In most of these dimensions, they also improved, though the improvement was small. Given that beginning teachers in the DAI study, on average, struggled the most to teach ambitiously in the instructional scaffolding dimensions (see chapter 3), the pattern across Roberto's PLATO scores suggests that guidance, especially from coaches who can work with beginning teachers directly in their classrooms, can assist novices in building some skills in scaffolding their students' content learning. His case also points to the role that conceptual and practical resources from teacher preparation might play in this development as well.

Nora

Nora, a graduate of Meadowlark's TPP, began teaching in what she described as a well-resourced suburban school. The school she taught in served a racially diverse student population; over half the students lived in poverty. She felt a close "fit" with her colleagues' "morals and beliefs." School administrators, mentors, coaches, and teachers provided her considerable support. In addition to Nora's having an extended orientation period for beginning teachers that familiarized her with the district curriculum and policies, Nora's school colleagues shared practical resources, provided instructional and classroom management guidance, and allayed the stress and self-doubts she experienced as a beginning teacher. They also encouraged her to determine whether and how she would use the resources they offered her.

Despite this encouragement, in year 1, Nora felt uncomfortable asserting her professional judgment. Because she was much younger than many of her colleagues, she felt reluctant to voice her perspectives or share her ideas with them. She described her lack of confidence in relation to her veteran colleagues as the major "challenge" of her first year. That year, she adopted many of her colleagues' teaching practices, especially in ELA, even when she did not agree with them.

While the district and school provided Nora with a plethora of resources, over time she anchored her ELA and mathematics instruction in resources from Meadowlark's TPP. Her use of these resources differed, however, across the two subjects. In ELA, she drew primarily on a practical resource, small-group reading instruction, from student teaching. In mathematics, she drew on practical resources from Meadowlark mathematics methods courses and student teaching, in particular, the number talks instructional routine. She also actively sought out and utilized district- and school-based practical, conceptual, and social resources to develop her skill enacting this routine more ambitiously.

ELA: Increased reliance on TPP practical resources Throughout her first three years of teaching, Nora drew increasingly on practical resources from her TPP experiences to develop her ELA instruction. This was a response, largely, to what she perceived as unclear district and school ELA curricular guidelines. The district and school provided teachers multiple ELA resources, including a phonemic awareness program, a process writing program, benchmark assessments, a textbook series, and a well-stocked book room. The district also mandated that teachers devote sixty to ninety minutes to reading workshop and forty to forty-five minutes to writing each day. In year 1, Nora reported that the district provided teachers "a lot of" professional development on the reader's workshop approach. Despite the availability of these resources, she felt that the district and school had "no reading curriculum." Teachers had "flexibility" to determine what and how they taught in ELA. Lacking the curricular guidelines she wanted, in year 1, she felt "overwhelmed" by the plethora of resources and described being "overloaded . . . with stuff to do." Developing her ELA instruction was "a lot of trial and error."

In year 1, Nora turned to her school colleagues to build her ELA instruction. Her first-grade colleagues provided guidance and shared teaching materials. In addition to a mentor teacher who "coach[ed] [her] through a lot of activities she does," her grade-level team planned ELA lessons together. Nora found the English as a Second Language

(ESL) teacher who worked with students in her classroom especially helpful. The ESL teacher provided "another set of eyes" that assisted her in assessing her students' reading fluency and supporting their reading and writing development. The ESL teacher remained a consistent source of guidance for Nora throughout her first three years of teaching.

Over time, Nora turned more to resources from her TPP to develop her ELA instruction. These included a gradual release model, the use of writing models, modeling reading strategies, and using turn-and-talks to facilitate text-based discussions. She increasingly centered her ELA instruction on small-group reading instruction, which she learned primarily from student teaching. Her cooperating teacher had devoted much of her ELA block to small-group instruction, and as a student teacher Nora facilitated small reading groups. Though the approach aligned with the district's reading workshop focus, she emphasized small reading group instruction because of "loving doing [them]" as a student teacher and because as a student teacher she attributed her students' growth in reading to the instructional routine.

During her first three years, Nora shifted more of her ELA block away from whole- class reading instruction because she felt small-group instruction allowed her to address the specific needs of students "at different levels," from those who struggled to those reading at or above grade level. Nora's own experiences as a student who found decoding and comprehension difficult reinforced her emphasis on small-group instruction. It allowed her to support students in her classroom who faced similar challenges. Small-group reading instruction also allowed Nora to monitor and respond to students' learning. During small-group instruction, she took notes on the reading skills students struggled with and planned ways to address them in subsequent groups. By year 3, she repeatedly confirmed her commitment to small-group reading instruction, frequently stating that she would "never not do guided reading."

As she gained more experience facilitating guided reading groups, Nora also found some school resources more helpful. She viewed the school's book room, which had an ample supply of leveled texts, as "a huge resource." Instead of being "overwhelmed" as in year 1, in year 2 she described "systematically" selecting texts that "were a good fit with [her] students." Small-group instruction thus served, in part, as a conceptual resource; it framed how she viewed the practical resources available in her school. Yet, Nora's grasp of the principles underlying small-group instruction seemed somewhat limited. Throughout her first three years she used the terms "guided reading," "small-group reading time," "small-group instruction," and "reader's workshop" interchangeably to describe what was, effectively, a guided reading routine in which she worked with small groups of similarly skilled students to build their fluency and comprehension as they read and discussed leveled texts.

In years 2 and 3, Nora used fewer ELA resources from her grade-level colleagues. She initially used the resources that these veteran colleagues shared with her when she moved to second grade in year 2. By year 3, however, she only loosely planned with her grade-level colleagues, who she felt used more whole-class ELA instruction than she did.

> I really, really like the small-group structure. . . . What I learned in student teaching, what I learned at Meadowlark . . . how I learned, is like where we're headed. And if I was a twenty-year teacher, I don't have the knowledge necessarily. So, I do so much small-group instruction in reading. So that's why a lot of what we do is different in reading. . . . Some of those more formal pieces, we will stick to the same schedule for that. But I am someone who if my students don't need two days on that, I'm not going to take two days on that. That's all about knowing your students. I have a lot more flexibility with that than I would say my teammates do.

Nora's comments reflect both her commitment to employing small-group reading instruction and to adapting her ELA instruction to her students' learning. They also illustrate how she constructed her ELA teaching identity as distinct from her more veteran colleagues' instruction. By year 3, she viewed her novice teacher status as a resource for teaching ELA rather than limiting her confidence or competence. She believed she possessed knowledge of instructional practices that her veteran colleagues did not. This knowledge, drawn largely from her student teaching experiences, enabled her to establish her ELA instruction in ways she believed better responded to her students' needs.

Mathematics: Expanding practical resources from TPP to teach more ambitiously Nora centrally developed her mathematics instruction based on resources from Meadowlark's TPP. She used these resources to enact and extend the district mathematics curriculum. The most important resource for her was the number talks instructional routine that she had developed a "passion" for in her mathematics methods courses and in student teaching after introducing the routine to her cooperating teacher. The routine had become her "little baby." In her first year of teaching, Nora introduced number talks to her grade-level team when the team struggled to engage their first graders in the solve-and-share component of the district's mathematics program. As she continued to use the routine in her mathematics teaching, she established herself as a resource for her colleagues. By year 2, other teachers came to her classroom to observe her teach. She reported her colleagues saying, "You need to go into Nora's room and watch how her kids have these conversations that you don't think second graders can do." By year 3, number talks had become central to Nora's identity as a mathematics teacher. When describing her mathematics instruction, she asserted, "If someone told me, 'Stop doing number talks,' I would be crushed. I would be like, 'No!'"

Nora also drew on her student teaching experiences to forge her mathematics instruction. As a student teacher, she attended professional development on the mathematics program that her current district had adopted and then used what she learned. The problem-based program focused on a lesson structure that included four components: solve-and-share, visual learning, guided practice, and independent practice. Because of her familiarity with the program, during her first three years of teaching, Nora felt "confident" utilizing the program and assisting her colleagues in using it as well. She also modified and adapted the district curriculum. While she followed the district pacing guide, she supplemented the curriculum with resources she found online and with the number talks routine, which she used to "deepen [students'] understanding" of mathematical procedures and concepts.

Nora did draw on school-based resources in mathematics, often to augment her use of the number talks routine. A district mathematics coach newly assigned to Nora's school in year 2 was central among them. While her veteran grade-level colleagues rejected the new coach, throughout years 2 and 3, she worked with the coach to expand her use of number talks. The coach helped Nora go beyond inviting students to share their thinking to engaging them in examining and deepening their understanding of their different problem-solving strategies. The coach assisted her in teaching her students to "respectfully disagree with each other" during number talks and helping her enact the district curriculum in "more innovative" ways.

Nora also used the teacher evaluation process as a resource for cultivating her skills enacting the number talks routine. In year 1, the principal gave her a "great score" on her observation of her mathematics teaching, boosting her confidence. "I had all of this stress. 'I don't think I know if this is what I'm supposed to be doing.' But it reassured me that this is correct. 'You're doing a good job and don't be so hard on yourself.'" The evaluation framework included a focus on "utilizing questions and having students question each other rather than the teacher instruct[ing]." In years 2 and 3, Nora focused on moving from "proficient" to "excellent" in this area. One of her year 2 teaching goals was to "make sure that [her]students were able to talk to each other academically and agree with each other and disagree with each other and question each other's thoughts." She attributed her "excellent" rating in this area in year 2 to her growing skill in "step[ping] back and challeng[ing] the kids to question each other." She used the district's evaluation framework as a conceptual resource that helped her use the number talks routine, a practical resource, more ambitiously.

Over time, Nora increasingly viewed her students' ideas as a resource for her mathematics teaching. Her efforts to engage her students in critically examining their thinking expanded her view of her students' capabilities. Teaching students to engage in discussions about their mathematical reasoning, "to disagree and agree with each other," had been "eye opening" for her. Through doing so, she "learned to sit back and watch and see, wow, they are really capable. . . . Some of these kids are super smart and know a lot and have background information and knowledge." As she learned more about her students' ideas, she also learned more about the difficulties some students faced in their lives outside of school. Nora initially found this emotionally upsetting. She struggled not to be "negative" with these students when they posed management challenges for her. As she paid more attention to students and their ideas, she gained a more complex understanding of her students and of her responsibilities to "hold them accountable for what they're capable of" while being a "positive force" in their lives.

In year 3, Nora struggled to identify how she could "transfer" students' substantive engagement in number talks to their performance on district summative assessments. She explained, "Our number talks always go really well. . . . I just wish that there was something I could do to really understand their thinking and without this summative assessment, where it's like, 'Okay we've done all these practice problems. Put this paper in front of you.' And then they tank on it. . . . I know that they're learning it because of the observations I'm making, but then how can I now transfer that into their work? . . . I struggle to find that piece."

Having developed her skill using the number talks routine, Nora experienced growing tensions between her observations of how the routine fostered her students' learning and her students' performance on the district assessment. She identified helping students transfer their learning between the two as an area for her own development and learning.

Finally, as in ELA, Nora established her identity as a mathematics teacher in relation to her grade-level colleagues. In years 2 and 3, she planned mathematics lessons with her grade-level team on an increasingly limited basis. The team shared resources aimed at meeting the expectations and timelines outlined in the district pacing guide. She felt, however, that her grade-level colleagues valued adhering to the pacing guide over responding to their students. In year 2, new to teaching second grade, she "wanted to do the program with fidelity towards my team." By year 3, she considered her students' specific learning needs first, noting, "Now I'm like, 'Okay, well, what do the kids need versus what do all second graders need?' . . . My instructional decisions are based on the kids I have." While Nora used the district pacing guide and mathematics program to plan her mathematics lessons, she adapted and modified both to meet her students' learning needs. She also used her colleagues' strict compliance with district curricular guidelines as a counter against which to construct her identity as a responsive mathematics teacher.

Nora's PLATO scores Table 4.4 reports Nora's scores in ELA and mathematics for year 1 through year 3 in the eleven PLATO dimensions. Similar to Jessica and Roberto, Nora had strong skills in managing student behavior and time to facilitate student learning. In ELA, her year 3 scores in the intellectual challenge and text-based instruction dimensions were among her highest and improved by over one point

TABLE 4.4 Nora's PLATO ELA and mathematics scores by dimension and year

PLATO domain: dimension	*ELA Y1*	*ELA Y2*	*ELA Y3*	*Math Y1*	*Math Y2*	*Math Y3*
Instructional scaffolding: modeling	1.58	2.25	2.25	**2.67**	**3.17**	**2.67**
instructional scaffolding: conceptual strategy use and instruction	1.13	1.58	1.33	1.33	1.42	**2.50**
Instructional scaffolding: procedural strategy use and instruction	1.42	1.42	1.33	2.33	**3.17**	2.42
Instructional scaffolding: feedback	2.02	2.17	2.17	2.08	2.00	2.25
Disciplinary demand: intellectual challenge	1.33	2.25	**2.50**	2.08	2.33	**2.67**
Disciplinary demand: classroom discourse	1.50	**2.50**	2.25	2.33	**2.58**	**2.67**
Disciplinary demand text-based instruction	1.33	2.25	**2.50**	X	X	X
Representations/organization of content: representation of content	2.48	**2.50**	2.17	**2.50**	**2.83**	**2.75**
Representations of content: purpose	2.37	2.08	**2.58**	**3.08**	**2.83**	**2.58**
Classroom environment: behavior management	**3.92**	**3.08**	**3.92**	**3.92**	**3.33**	**3.75**
Classroom environment: time management	**3.60**	**3.25**	**3.33**	**3.50**	**3.50**	**3.25**

Note: We consider PLATO dimension scores of 2.5 or higher as moving toward more ambitious teaching. We bolded those scores accordingly.

on a four-point scale between year 1 and year 3. Her other highest scores were in the classroom discourse dimension in year 2, and in the representation of content and purpose dimensions in year 2 and year 3, respectively. Her scores in the instructional scaffolding dimensions remained low across the three years. Nora shaped her ELA instruction largely around the small-group reading instruction routine she learned in student teaching, focusing her use of school-based practical resources around it. The PLATO scores suggest that while her use of these resources did not assist her in cultivating her skills scaffolding students' ELA knowledge and skills, it did assist her in developing some skill assigning ELA tasks that sometimes engaged students in interpreting and producing authentic texts and in building students' ideas through ELA-related conversations, though, again, inconsistently. Her use of the resources also seemed to help her build some skill explaining ELA concepts and procedures and articulating ELA learning goals, though, again, inconsistently.

Nora's PLATO scores in mathematics were among the highest in the DAI study. In contrast to her ELA PLATO scores, her highest scores, all roughly three points on PLATO's four-point scale, were in the modeling, procedural strategy use and instruction, and purpose dimensions. She demonstrated skill in teaching more ambitiously in these dimensions. Her scores in conceptual strategy use and instruction, intellectual challenge, classroom discourse, and representations and organization of content further indicate that Nora was developing her skills in these dimensions, as well. Taken together, her PLATO scores suggest that Nora's use of the number talks routine from her TPP and her efforts to focus her learning on the routine as she taught with the district's mathematics curriculum, worked with the mathematics coach's guidance, and attended to her students' ideas helped her cultivate her skills enacting several ambitious teaching practices in mathematics.

DISCUSSION

Jessica, Roberto, and Nora forged their teaching practices in ELA and mathematics as they made sense of, selected, and modified conceptual, practical, and social resources available from their experiences as students, their teacher preparation programs, and the districts and schools where they began their teaching careers. Whether and how they used these resources depended on their beliefs about teaching and learning, their sense of their own and their colleagues' professional competence, their students' learning, and their emotional responses to and investment in their work. As they utilized the different resources, these beginning teachers cultivated their skills enacting more ambitious practices in mathematics and ELA in some instructional dimensions, though they struggled to do so in other dimensions. The cases offer several insights for teacher preparation and induction programs.

First, the cases illustrate the complex ways that beginning teachers take up and utilize conceptual and practical resources from teacher preparation. Jessica, Roberto, and Nora all viewed these resources as foundational to their instruction. Yet, how they used these resources varied across the three teachers and across mathematics and ELA. Though they graduated from the same TPP, Jessica and Roberto drew very different types of resources from it. Both teachers taught in districts that had well-delineated ELA and mathematics curricula. Jessica drew specific conceptual and practical resources from Cardinal's TPP to develop her ELA and mathematics instruction as she taught with the district curricula. She viewed the TPP resources as explicitly aligned with school- and district-based conceptual and practical resources in both subjects, and school-based social resources in ELA. As a result, Jessica felt well prepared by Cardinal's TPP to teach both mathematics and ELA.

For Roberto, the prescriptive nature of the district ELA curriculum, combined with his initial lack of confidence and a felt sense of his vulnerability as an untenured novice led him to focus more singularly on employing the curriculum's practical resources rather than drawing actively on teacher preparation resources. Roberto did employ conceptual resources from teacher preparation more explicitly in mathematics. The resources assisted him in teaching the district's mathematics curriculum with its focus on multiple problem-solving strategies, a focus supported by the district mathematics coach but resisted by his colleagues.

Similar to Jessica, Nora drew directly on instructional practices she had encountered in her TPP to forge her ELA and mathematics instruction. Rather than focus her instructional development on district curricula and other school resources as Jessica did, Nora centered her use of district and school resources on the resources she took from Meadowlark's TPP. In ELA, Nora responded to what she perceived as a lack of curricular guidelines and her colleagues' overemphasis on whole-class instruction by centering her instruction on the small-group reading instruction routine that she learned primarily in student teaching. Although she became increasingly committed to the practice, her understanding of its underlying principles seemed limited.

In mathematics, Nora centered her teaching on the number talks instructional routine she had learned about and practiced in her mathematics methods courses and brought into her student teaching. She also actively sought out and utilized district and school social and practical resources to cultivate her skill utilizing the instructional routine. As she did so, school administrators and colleagues recognized Nora's competence as a mathematics teacher. Her drive and ability to integrate practical, conceptual, and social resources from teacher preparation and in her district and school assisted her in developing her skill enacting more ambitious instructional practices in mathematics across several instructional dimensions, especially modeling, procedural strategy use and instruction, and purpose.

The cases thus illustrate how teacher preparation can provide beginning teachers conceptual and practical resources with which to build a foundation for more ambitious teaching and point to the benefits of practice-based teacher education for assisting novices' development of ambitious instruction. Practice-based teacher education centrally aims to cultivate teacher candidates' abilities to skillfully and knowledgeably enact a small set of core teaching practices that support ambitious student learning and are foundational for novice teachers' subsequent professional development.[11] Nora gained knowledge about and fluency in using the number talks routine to elicit students' mathematical thinking, a core teaching practice, through her teacher preparation experiences. This enabled her to go beyond enacting the district mathematics curriculum to extending it. She was also able to more actively shape the guidance the mathematics coach provided her, focusing it on expanding her use of the number talks routine to deepen students' understanding of mathematical concepts and procedures. The opportunities to build her knowledge of and fluency in enacting practices that elicited and expanded her students' mathematical thinking not only helped Nora teach more ambitiously but also contributed to her sense of agency and professional competence.

While practice-based teacher education focuses on building teacher candidates' abilities to enact ambitious teaching practices, as Pam Grossman and her colleagues assert, it "integrates work on developing skills with work on developing the knowledge and judgement required to put those skills to use when working with students."[12] Conceptual resources remain essential in practice-based teacher education even as it refocuses the teacher education curriculum on practice. The cases illustrate how these resources can support beginning teachers in employing and learning from district- and school-based resources. Ensuring that novice teachers develop ambitious instructional practices requires integrating conceptual and practical resources in ways that enable novices to understand how *and* why they might use the practices to foster their students' learning.

Though Jessica, Roberto, and Nora all utilized at least some resources from teacher preparation to assist them in teaching with the practical resources related to their districts' curricula in both ELA and mathematics, their PLATO scores suggest that they were not able to teach the curricula in more ambitious ways in both subjects and across the different PLATO dimensions. Beginning teachers, such as Jessica, Roberto, and Nora, spend considerable time and effort becoming familiar with and learning how to teach district and/or school curricula.[13]

These materials and teachers' interpretations of them play a pivotal role in shaping teachers' instruction.[14] In addition, as the cases illustrate, beginning teachers encounter numerous practical resources from their colleagues who share their teaching materials and lessons with them.

Jessica's, Roberto's, and Nora's cases point to the potential benefits of providing teacher candidates structured opportunities to critically assess curricular and instructional materials for their intellectual challenge and to practice modifying and extending them to increase their rigor. This includes modeling how candidates can use the materials in intellectually challenging ways and providing candidates scaffolded opportunities to compare how different materials structure students' engagement with content and the educative features they provide for teachers.[15]

It also includes providing candidates opportunities to practice enacting specific ambitious instructional practices while using the curricular materials in their coursework and student teaching. Such opportunities might be particularly helpful to beginning teachers, such as Jessica, who had few social resources to assist her in utilizing the extensive teacher's guide that accompanied the mathematics program her district built its mathematics curriculum around. They could also be helpful to beginning teachers such as Roberto, who felt compelled to comply with the curriculum because of his novice status.

The cases also illustrate how the alignment of the resources that districts and schools make available shapes beginning teachers' development of their instructional practices, including more ambitious practices. Jessica, Roberto, and Nora all began their careers in districts and schools that offered a plethora of practical resources for teaching ELA and mathematics. Yet Nora, especially in ELA, felt overwhelmed by these resources. She was unable to discern a clear framework or a shared set of practices in the guidance and materials offered by the district and her school colleagues. In her first year, perceiving that the district and school lacked an ELA curriculum, Nora built her English instruction largely through trial and error and struggled to teach ambitiously. In her second and third years, she turned increasingly to forging her ELA instruction on her own.

In contrast, in mathematics Roberto received guidance from a coach on how to utilize the district curriculum to differentiate his lessons, elicit student reasoning, and facilitate students' use of multiple problem-solving strategies. Though he taught procedural strategies inconsistently, he built some skills in this dimension which, as chapter 3 shows, nearly all beginning teachers in the DAI study found challenging. Similarly, Jessica's district provided teachers with professional development and coaches who offered guidance aligned with the district's ELA curriculum. These resources, taken together, helped Jessica deepen her knowledge of the district's ELA curriculum and focus her ELA instruction on a shared set of instructional approaches and routines. Her PLATO ELA scores were highest in the disciplinary demand and representations and organization of content domains. These domains primarily focus on instructional practices that teachers use to establish learning goals, maintain their intellectual challenge, and clarify the content of the tasks they assign. The alignment of district and school ELA material and social resources assisted Jessica in learning how to teach tasks specified in the district's ELA curriculum more ambitiously.

The alignment among district and school material and social resources provided Roberto and Jessica consistent messages and a set of shared practices upon which to build their mathematics and ELA instruction, respectively. Research has found that this kind of coherence can enhance the quality of beginning teachers' induction experiences as it helps novices forge more productive relationships with their colleagues, mentors, and school administrators.[16] Our cases suggest that it might also assist novice teachers in building more ambitious teaching practices. As they design and enact induction programs, districts and schools might consider how the mentoring, coaching, and orientations they provide beginning teachers convey a coherent vision of quality instruction aligned with district and school curricular materials. Further, districts and schools could prepare mentors to support beginning teachers' enactment of the instructional practices associated with this vision.[17] As our case studies suggest, supporting novice teachers' development of ambitious instructional practices requires considering how their induction into the profession is situated within school and district instructional systems and shaped by their coherence.

The cases further point to the complex relationships that beginning teachers can have with their school colleagues and how these relationships can shape their instructional development. While all three novices had generally positive relationships with their colleagues, Roberto and Nora experienced some tensions with them. These related to differences in instructional practices and, in Roberto's case, also in views of students marginalized by poverty and racism. These tensions and the beginning teachers' responses to them aided them in building both their teaching identities and more ambitious instructional practices. Roberto, the only male Teacher of Color in his school and a graduate of the district he taught in, resisted his colleagues' deficit views of students, many of whom were Students of Color and living in poverty. Maintaining his belief in and commitment to his students' learning reflected both the identities he shared with his students and his identity as a student-centered teacher. He also separated himself from his colleagues' resistance to teaching multiple problem-solving strategies in mathematics. Doing so enabled him to continue to build his skill in some dimensions of instructional scaffolding.

Nora more explicitly rejected her more veteran colleagues' instructional practices in both ELA and mathematics. As she did so, she constructed an identity as a responsive teacher who readily modified district and school curricular materials. This allowed her to attend more closely to her students' learning, which, in turn, helped her both recognize her students' strengths and capabilities and identify areas for improving her instruction, especially in mathematics.

The cases thus suggest that while guidance and sharing from colleagues can assist beginning teachers in teaching more ambitiously, teacher preparation and induction programs might also consider how they can support novice teachers in critically evaluating these resources. This might also include working with beginning teachers in preservice and induction programs to recognize and resist deficit views of students as they build their knowledge of and fluency enacting ambitious instructional practices that provide novices insight into student thinking.

Finally, the cases point to the role that beginning teachers' emotional engagement in their work plays in their instructional development. The three teachers all described experiencing some stress and uncertainty as novice teachers. These feelings led some, at times, to comply with policies and guidance from administrators and colleagues that they felt ran counter to their beliefs about teaching and learning. At the same time, all three novices expressed their "love" and/or "passion" for teaching ELA and/or mathematics, and for specific instructional practices as well. Jessica and Nora, in particular, became increasingly committed to particular approaches and instructional routines in their first three years of teaching, pointing to the consequential nature of these years for teachers' instructional development. Finally, the three beginning teachers also expressed joy in their students' growth and learning.

As teacher preparation and induction programs seek to assist beginning teachers to teach more ambitiously, it is important to consider the emotional dimensions of this work and to help novice teachers in sustaining their passion for teaching as they encounter its demands and challenges. Teaching ambitiously both requires and allows teachers to learn more about students' thinking and their understanding of disciplinary concepts, practices, and questions. Enabling children and young people to risk sharing their thinking and what they know and don't know with their peers and teachers requires that teachers learn more about their students, promote their social and emotional learning, and foster positive relationships with and between them. This involves emotional work. As Nora noted, as she attended more to her students' thinking, she learned more about her students' lives, including the difficulties some faced. When these students posed some management challenges for her, she struggled to remain positive and to maintain high expectations for their learning. Assisting beginning teachers to teach ambitiously will require acknowledging and helping novice teachers understand and engage in this emotional work in sustainable and productive ways.

CHAPTER 5

Implications for Teacher Preparation Programs, School Districts, and Researchers

Efforts by policy makers and educators alike to improve educational opportunities for all students in US schools have focused attention on how beginning teachers can learn to teach ambitiously. Such attention has led, in turn, to increased scrutiny of university-based teacher preparation programs. In the proceeding chapters, we have drawn on data from the Development of Ambitious Instruction (DAI) study to explore the nature of novice teachers' development of ambitious instructional practices in mathematics and English language arts (ELA) and to identify the types of learning opportunities and resources provided by preparation programs that contribute to it. We further examined how beginning teachers made sense of and took up resources available in the schools where they started their careers. Throughout, we considered the ways in which novice teachers' individual characteristics, goals, and beliefs about teaching and learning mattered to their instructional development within and across the two subject areas.

In this chapter, we draw across the analyses we presented in previous chapters to highlight key findings from the DAI study regarding how teacher preparation programs can build beginning teachers' knowledge and skills to teach ambitiously. We then explore implications for teacher education programs and for elementary schools and school districts. As our case studies in chapter 4 show, the resources available in elementary schools play a critical role in how novice teachers make use of learning opportunities that their preparation programs provided them in their teaching. Both preparation programs and elementary schools need to consider how they can assist beginning teachers in leveraging the knowledge and skills that they develop in their teacher preparation programs and the schools where they begin their careers to cultivate more ambitious teaching practices.

Finally, we consider implications for future research. During their first years of teaching, novices transition from being students in university preparation programs to being professionals in elementary schools with responsibilities to students and their families, colleagues, administrators, and the broader school community. Determining what teacher preparation experiences matter to beginning teachers' instructional development amid this complex transition poses several challenges for researchers. Drawing on our experiences conducting the DAI study, we propose ways to address these challenges and build the knowledge base needed to ensure that novice teachers are able to provide their students with rigorous and equitable learning opportunities.

LESSONS LEARNED FROM THE DAI STUDY

We designed the DAI study to follow elementary teacher candidates from five university-based teacher preparation programs as they moved from student teaching into their first two to three years of teaching. We aimed to identify teacher preparation learning experiences that assist beginning elementary teachers in enacting ambitious instructional practices. Our analyses of survey, interview, and classroom observation data yielded insights into novice elementary teachers' development of these practices as well as the learning opportunities and resources they encountered in their teacher preparation programs and schools that supported such development. Because beginning teachers make sense of and utilize these opportunities and resources in light of their own goals and beliefs, we also considered how novice teachers' individual characteristics seemed to affect whether and how they taught more or less ambitiously. In the next sections, we present key findings in each of these areas.

Elementary teachers' development of ambitious instructional practices in their first and second years: Areas of growth and continued challenge

The first two years of teaching are consequential. During this time, teachers establish many of the instructional practices they will use throughout their careers. Like most teachers, the beginning teachers in our DAI study struggled to teach ambitiously. They did, however, more readily develop their skills enacting some ambitious practices than others. In both their first and second years of full-time teaching, novice teachers' Protocol for Language Arts Teaching Observation (PLATO) scores in the classroom environment domain, on average, were in the upper half of the four-point PLATO scale. On average, the beginning teachers in the DAI study entered teaching able to manage student behavior and time in ways that maintained students' engagement in learning activities. In contrast, their PLATO scores in the instructional domains (i.e., disciplinary demand, representations and organization of content, and instructional scaffolding) were, on average, in the lower half of the PLATO scale.

Although the beginning teachers we observed struggled overall to enact ambitious instructional practices, they did teach more ambitiously in their second year. On average, the novice teachers' overall PLATO composite and instructional composite scores in both mathematics and ELA demonstrated small but statistically significant improvements from their first to their second year of teaching. This reflected, in part, beginning teachers' improvement in the classroom environment domain. The teachers' mathematics and ELA PLATO scores also improved significantly in the disciplinary demand domain, with much of this growth in the intellectual challenge dimension. In year 2, the novice teachers more frequently engaged students in learning tasks that involved analysis, interpretation, and idea generation in both subjects. They also improved in the representations and organization of content domain, though only in ELA. Much of this growth was in the purpose dimension, indicating that the beginning teachers became more proficient at communicating ELA learning objectives and aligning instructional activities with those objectives.

The novice teachers' development of more ambitious practices in the instructional scaffolding domain was more limited. Their PLATO scores in this domain showed little improvement between their first and second years. We did find very small but significant improvement in the conceptual strategy use and instruction dimension in ELA and the feedback dimension in mathematics. Notably, the beginning teachers' PLATO scores in the feedback dimension in ELA and mathematics were among their highest dimension-level scores across the instructional domains. This suggests that novice teachers might be able to more readily develop their skills providing students productive feedback. Building their skills in modeling and explicitly teaching students how and why to use conceptual or procedural strategies to complete ELA and mathematics tasks is likely to require more time and more targeted support during both initial preparation and the early years of teaching.

Teacher preparation opportunities to learn and beginning elementary teachers' enactment of ambitious instruction: A complex picture

The DAI study centrally aimed to identify learning opportunities in teacher preparation programs that were associated with beginning teachers' enactment of ambitious instructional practices in mathematics and ELA. The analyses we presented in previous chapters, taken together, provide a complex picture of how teacher preparation is associated with and shapes novice elementary teachers' instruction. They shed light on the ambitious practices that different learning opportunities and resources in teacher preparation can assist beginning teachers to enact both within and across mathematics and ELA and their first years of teaching.

Elementary teacher candidate perceptions of teacher preparation opportunities to learn Our analysis of the opportunities to learn that the five preparation programs in the DAI study provided to beginning teachers rests on the novices' perceptions of these opportunities that they reported on our Elementary Teacher Candidate survey. Though this provides only a partial picture of the learning opportunities the programs offered, candidates' perceptions of these opportunities are important. Whether the opportunities to learn that preparation programs offer candidates matter to beginning teachers' instruction depends on how the teacher candidates make sense of these opportunities.

We focused specifically on three types of opportunities to learn: general methods, strategies to teach diverse learners, and ambitious instructional practices in mathematics and ELA. We found that, on average, teacher candidates in the five preparation programs reported having opportunities to discuss and try out general principles and methods of instruction, such as lesson planning and motivating students, and strategies for teaching diverse learners. We did find some within-program variation in candidates' perceptions of these opportunities, especially in relation to the latter. Within the different preparation programs, teacher candidates reported that the amount of time and depth spent on learning strategies for working with diverse learners varied greatly; for some candidates, these strategies were touched on only briefly, while others felt they had extensive opportunities to learn about them.

The candidates' perceptions of their opportunities to learn about and try out ambitious teaching strategies in mathematics and ELA varied less within programs. We asked candidates to report on their opportunities to learn twelve ambitious instructional practices in each subject. Across the five programs, candidates consistently reported that they had opportunities to try using nearly all of the strategies with elementary students during student teaching. In contrast, though candidates' survey responses varied across the programs, they reported having opportunities to learn roughly half of the twelve strategies in each subject through examining video or written cases or trying them out with their peers in their methods courses. Overall, the beginning teachers felt that as candidates, they had more opportunities to build their skills enacting ambitious instructional practices in both mathematics and ELA during student teaching than in their methods courses. As we show in the next section, this mattered for their development of more ambitious instruction early in their careers.

Teacher preparation opportunities to learn and the ambitiousness of beginning teachers' first- and second-year mathematics and ELA instruction We drew on both the Elementary Teacher Candidate survey and our observations of beginning teachers' mathematics and ELA lessons to examine associations between the different types of opportunities to learn that candidates reported receiving in their preparation programs and their enactment of ambitious instructional practices in the different PLATO domains in their first and second years of teaching. We found that in their first year of teaching, novices in the DAI study who reported having more extensive opportunities to learn general principles and methods of instruction in their preparation programs enacted more ambitious teaching practices in the disciplinary demand and instructional scaffolding domains in both mathematics and ELA. Although, on average, the beginning teachers' first-year PLATO scores were low in both domains, candidates' learning about and trying out general methods of lesson planning and motivating students, for example, provided a foundation for them to elicit and respond to students' ideas and to engage students in intellectually challenging learning tasks as first-year teachers. These opportunities also assisted them in providing more educative feedback and modeling and explicitly teaching conceptual and procedural strategies more skillfully than their peers who did not report such opportunities.

We did not find statistically significant associations between teacher preparation opportunities to learn general methods and beginning teachers' second-year PLATO scores in either disciplinary demand or instructional scaffolding. As we noted previously, novice teachers in the DAI study did make small but statistically significant improvements in disciplinary demand but not in instructional scaffolding in either mathematics or ELA. Further, they appeared to have struggled the most enacting practices related to instructional scaffolding. Taken together, our findings thus suggest that opportunities to learn general methods in teacher preparation might provide beginning teachers with a stronger foundation for cultivating their skills in the disciplinary demand domain than in the instructional scaffolding domain, especially in their first years of teaching. Disciplinary demand includes engaging students in tasks that involve interpretation and analysis as well as eliciting and responding to students' ideas. Enacting these practices can involve strategies for planning tasks and discourse moves that teachers can apply across subject areas.

Instructional scaffolding, in contrast, involves teachers modeling and teaching their students how and why to use conceptual and procedural strategies to build students' content knowledge and skills. Doing so requires that beginning teachers have strong understandings of mathematical and ELA concepts and of the subject-specific rules, algorithms, or formulae needed to engage in mathematics and ELA tasks. Novice teachers are likely to need opportunities in teacher preparation and throughout their first years of teaching to deepen their content and pedagogical content knowledge in order to build these understandings and cultivate their instructional scaffolding skills. Learning general methods as teacher candidates might assist beginning teachers in introducing or prompting their students to use conceptual or procedural strategies productively. But they do not appear to be sufficient to assist novices in further cultivating their skills scaffolding their students' deeper understanding of subject matter concepts and practices.

Beyond the first-year association between opportunities to learn general methods and beginning teachers' PLATO scores in disciplinary demand and instructional scaffolding in both subjects, our findings suggest that teacher preparation opportunities appear to have more impact on the ambitiousness of beginning teachers' instruction in mathematics than in ELA, especially in their first year of teaching. We found that opportunities to try out and receive feedback on ambitious mathematics teaching strategies in student teaching and to learn strategies to teach diverse students were associated with both more and less ambitious mathematics instruction in different PLATO domains in the first year of teaching, respectively. Novice teachers who reported having more extensive opportunities to try out and receive feedback on ambitious mathematics teaching strategies in student teaching had higher first-year PLATO mathematics scores in the instructional scaffolding and representations and organization of content domains. The same opportunities, however, were negatively associated with their scores in classroom environment. Beginning teachers who reported having more extensive opportunities to learn how to teach diverse learners, conversely, had high PLATO mathematics scores in classroom environment but lower scores in all the instructional domains. Though notably, in year 2, the same teachers had higher scores in instructional scaffolding in mathematics.

These findings point to the complex relationship between teacher preparation opportunities to learn, classroom management, and ambitious instruction in mathematics. When elementary teachers who had opportunities in student teaching to try out ambitious mathematics teaching practices enact these practices during their first year of teaching, they might focus less on managing student behavior and time and might encounter some challenges doing so. In contrast, novices appeared to employ the strategies to teach diverse learners that they learned in teacher preparation to positively manage student behavior during mathematics lessons. These strategies did not, however, assist them in teaching mathematics more ambitiously until their second year, when they appeared to be better able to employ these strategies to improve their strategy instruction.

In ELA, our analyses raise questions about how elementary candidates' opportunities to learn ambitious instructional practices in student teaching and in their courses assist them in learning to teach more ambitiously. Candidates who reported having more extensive opportunities to try out and receive feedback on ambitious ELA instructional strategies during student teaching generally had higher PLATO ELA scores in the representations and organization of content domain in their second teaching year, while candidates who reported having the same opportunities in their courses had lower scores in this domain. As we noted earlier, the elementary candidates in the DAI study reported trying out roughly half as many ambitious practices in their courses than they did in their student teaching. It may be that they had fewer opportunities in their courses to develop their skills explaining ELA concepts or articulating learning goals for the ELA tasks they teach than they did in student teaching. Our findings suggest that such opportunities might be especially salient to assisting beginning elementary teachers as they forge their ELA instruction.

Teacher and school characteristics and novice elementary teachers' enactment of ambitious instruction In the DAI study, we also examined associations between teacher and school characteristics and beginning teachers' enactment of ambitious instruction. Several had statistically significant associations with the ambitiousness of beginning teachers' mathematics and ELA instruction. These included beginning teachers' college GPA, their self-efficacy with regard to teaching mathematics and ELA, and the percentage of students living in poverty that their schools enrolled.

Research has consistently found that teachers' academic ability is positively associated with their effectiveness as measured by student achievement outcomes.[1] The analyses we presented in chapter 3 found a similar association with beginning teachers' enactment of ambitious instructional practices. First-year teachers with higher GPAs had higher scores in the instructional scaffolding and representations and organization of content domains in mathematics and in all three instructional domains in ELA. Higher undergraduate GPA was negatively associated, however, with first-year teachers' classroom environment scores in mathematics and second-year teachers' classroom environment scores in ELA.

Our analyses of beginning teachers' self-efficacy and their enactment of ambitious instruction further reflect this complex association between classroom management and content instruction. We found that first-year teachers' self-efficacy had positive associations with PLATO classroom environment scores in both mathematics and ELA but negative associations with PLATO scores in the instructional domains. Further, second-year teachers' self-efficacy had negative associations with classroom environment scores in ELA. While first-year teachers with high self-efficacy had strong behavior and time management skills, this did not necessarily lead them to teach more ambitiously. Indeed, our findings suggest that focusing on managing student behavior and time might impede novice teachers' efforts to employ more ambitious teaching practices, which pose more management risks and challenges than less ambitious teaching practices.

Finally, we considered the association between the percentage of students living in poverty within a school and beginning teachers' enactment of ambitious instructional practice. We found that, on average, first-year teachers who taught in high-poverty schools received lower scores for disciplinary demand in mathematics and ELA and that second-year teachers who taught in such schools generally received lower ratings for instructional scaffolding in ELA. These findings suggest that in their first year of teaching, novices in high-poverty schools struggled to maintain students' engagement in intellectually rigorous tasks. They continued to struggle their second year to enact more ambitious scaffolding practices in ELA. On the one hand, these findings suggest that beginning teachers might lower their expectations for students living in poverty. On the other hand, we did not find that novice teachers who began their careers in high-poverty schools encountered more classroom management problems or that, on the whole, they found teaching ambitiously significantly more challenging than their peers in lower-poverty schools. In their second year, their skills engaging their students in more challenging learning tasks were similar to those of their peers' teaching in lower-poverty schools.

Learning from the cases of Jessica, Roberto, and Nora: The role of teacher preparation and school-based resources in beginning teachers' development of ambitious instruction Given the complexity of beginning teachers' development of ambitious instructional practices, in chapter 4, we explored this development in more depth through the cases of three novice elementary teachers whom we followed through their first three years of teaching. In particular, we examined how the three teachers, Jessica, Roberto, and Nora, utilized resources from their teacher preparation programs and the schools where they began their teaching careers to forge their mathematics and ELA instruction. The three novices' PLATO composite scores in mathematics and ELA began or became among the more ambitious in the DAI study. Their cases, taken together, illuminate the role that teacher preparation learning opportunities and resources can play in supporting beginning teachers' development of ambitious teaching practices as they work with their students and their school colleagues. In particular, the cases show how novice teachers' perceptions of these opportunities and resources and their goals, or their personal sense, fundamentally shape whether and how they draw on their preparation experiences in their first years of teaching.

Similar to the larger sample of beginning teachers, Jessica's, Roberto's, and Nora's PLATO scores in the disciplinary demand domain were among their highest across the instructional domains and dimensions. For Roberto, though, this was only in ELA. Disciplinary demand includes the dimensions of intellectual challenge, classroom discourse, and, in ELA, text-based instruction. It focuses on the intellectual rigor of the activities that teachers assign their students. Given that district and school curricula often shape if not determine the activities that novice teachers assign their students, beginning teachers are likely to improve their abilities to engage students at a more intellectually challenging level as they strengthen their understanding of and skills teaching with school curricula.

At the same time, our cases show that beginning teachers can leverage teacher preparation learning opportunities and resources to cultivate their skills in the disciplinary demand domain. In their first years of teaching, Jessica and Roberto, in particular, focused on learning their district's curricula in mathematics and ELA and centered their teaching on them. Although Jessica and Roberto both graduated in the same cohort from Cardinal University's teacher preparation program, they made use in very different ways of the learning opportunities and resources it provided them. Roberto believed that his experiences in Cardinal's preparation program provided him a foundation to build his identity and practice as a "student-centered" teacher. He seldom reported, however, drawing on specific learning opportunities or resources from the program in his mathematics or ELA instruction. Roberto's PLATO composite scores were more ambitious than those of most of the other novices in the DAI study. His scores in the instructional domains and dimensions did not, however, reach the levels of ambitiousness that Jessica's did in ELA or Nora's did in mathematics.

Unlike Roberto, Jessica actively drew on the conceptual and practical resources she encountered in Cardinal's preparation program. Jessica's ELA PLATO scores in the intellectual challenge and text-based instruction dimensions in the disciplinary demand domain were ambitious; they reached or were near the upper half of the PLATO scale. They indicate that Jessica was able to provide her students instructional activities that frequently involved them in analysis, interpretations, inferencing, or idea generation and allowed them to engage with or produce authentic texts. Jessica developed her skills in these dimensions as she deepened her understanding of her district's ELA curriculum and its workshop approach through both district-provided professional development and the collaborative planning and analyses of student learning that she engaged in with her school colleagues.

Jessica attributed much of the growth in her ELA instruction to these school-based learning opportunities. She also viewed the opportunities to learn about and try out components of an ELA workshop approach provided in her ELA methods courses at Cardinal University as foundational to her learning. Jessica felt that these opportunities gave her an advantage as a beginning teacher. They enabled her to strengthen her own understanding of and skill engaging students in interpreting and producing authentic texts, and they allowed her to serve as a resource for her more veteran colleagues. In her first years of teaching, Jessica actively drew on the conceptual and practical resources from her teacher preparation opportunities as she utilized the conceptual and practical resources available in her school to forge her ELA instruction.

Jessica's, Roberto's, and Nora's cases also reflect the struggles and possibilities that the beginning teachers in the larger DAI sample encountered in relation to building their teaching practices in the instructional scaffolding domain. Similar to the larger sample, Jessica's and Roberto's PLATO scores were, on the whole, among the lowest in this domain. In mathematics, however, Roberto's score in the procedural strategy use and instruction dimension was among one of his highest and improved each year. Roberto reported that learning in his teacher preparation program about how and why to support students' use of multiple approaches to solving mathematical problems enabled him to build his skills teaching the district's mathematics curriculum, despite his colleagues' resistance to the curriculum. This was one of the few examples of Roberto's utilizing specific teacher preparation learning opportunities and conceptual resources in his teaching.

Nora's case further illustrates how beginning teachers can draw on learning opportunities and employ resources from teacher preparation to enact more ambitious teaching practices. This was especially true in mathematics. While Nora's PLATO scores in the instructional scaffolding domain in ELA were low, her mathematics scores in the modeling and conceptual and procedural strategy use and instruction dimensions of this domain were among her highest. Unlike most of the beginning teachers in the DAI study, many of Nora's PLATO scores in these dimensions across her first years of teaching were at or near the upper half of the PLATO scale. Nora centered her mathematics instruction on the number talks routine she had learned in her mathematics methods course at Meadowlark, a routine she had brought into both her student teaching and her first years of full-time teaching.

Like Jessica and Roberto, Nora spent significant effort learning how to teach the district mathematics curriculum, but she actively sought out and found ways to integrate the number talks routine into the curriculum. In her second year of teaching, this created some tensions with her colleagues, whom she felt focused too much on following the curriculum rather than addressing their students' strengths and learning needs. She also worked to engage with the district's mathematics coach and the district's teacher evaluation system to deepen and expand her knowledge of and use of the routine. As she did so, Nora developed her skills in eliciting and expanding students' thinking about and understanding of mathematics concepts and procedures.

Notably, Nora also utilized resources from teacher preparation in her ELA instruction, but they did not appear to have supported her development of ambitious instructional scaffolding practices in that subject. Nora focused her early-career ELA instruction on a small-group instruction model that she learned while student teaching. She did not, however, report also developing her knowledge of this model in her teacher preparation courses. Her case points, again, to the potential benefits of coordinating teacher candidates' opportunities to build their knowledge and fluency enacting particular instructional routines across university coursework and school-based placements.

Jessica's, Roberto's, and Nora's cases thus demonstrate the ways in which teacher preparation opportunities to learn as well as resources available to beginning elementary teachers can assist them in enacting more ambitious teaching practices as they work with their students and school colleagues. At the same time, the cases also show how beginning teachers' perceptions of these learning opportunities and resources critically shape the ways in which these novices make sense of and take them up in their teaching. Their cases point to the value of both teacher preparation programs and elementary schools supporting beginning teachers in recognizing and utilizing the range of resources and learning opportunities available to them to cultivate their emergent teaching skills.

IMPLICATIONS FOR ELEMENTARY TEACHER PREPARATION PROGRAMS AND SCHOOL DISTRICTS

Teaching ambitiously requires that teachers possess deep content and pedagogical content knowledge and the skills to employ this knowledge in ways that facilitate their students' learning. The findings of our DAI study, similar to those presented in other studies of ambitious instruction, indicate that learning to teaching ambitiously is likely to take several years for most novices.[2] At the same time, our findings show that beginning teachers can take small but significant steps toward teaching more ambitiously and that teacher preparation learning opportunities can assist them in this work. We consider the implications of these findings for both the teacher preparation programs and the schools in which elementary teachers learn to teach.

First, our findings suggest that beginning elementary teachers seem to develop their skills enacting some ambitious instructional practices more than others. The novice teachers that we observed for the DAI study demonstrated statistically significant improvement in disciplinary demand between their first and second years of teaching in both mathematics and ELA; in particular, much of this change was in the intellectual challenge dimension. In general, beginning teachers' skills maintaining the intellectual challenge of the tasks they assign their students are often closely related to school- or district-based curricula in mathematics and ELA. As the cases we presented in chapter 4 illustrate, district curricula can strongly shape teachers' decisions about tasks and learning objectives.[3] As novice teachers gain more knowledge of and experience teaching with district and school curricular and instructional materials, they can better sustain the cognitive demand of tasks during mathematics and ELA lessons and communicate their learning objectives to students.

Our findings suggest that providing opportunities to learn about general teaching methods and general principles of instruction during preservice preparation seemed to provide a strong foundation for beginning teachers' developing their skills in this instructional dimension. Given the centrality of district- and school-based curricula to novice teachers' instruction, teacher preparation programs might further support beginning teachers' development in this dimension by providing their candidates opportunities to critically assess curricular materials for their intellectual challenge and to practice modifying or extending curricular materials to increase their rigor. This includes modeling how candidates can use the materials in intellectually challenging ways;[4] it also includes providing them scaffolded opportunities to compare how different materials structure students' engagement with content and the educative features they provide for teachers.[5] These kinds of preparation experiences could be especially powerful for novices who have limited opportunities to critically assess curricular materials with their colleagues or have limited support from instructional coaches to teach with the materials in ways that engage students in intellectually challenging tasks.

In schools, teachers' grade-level planning teams can be vital sites for supporting beginning teachers' skills engaging their students in intellectually challenging tasks. For these groups to be supportive, however, teachers need to expand their conversations beyond concerns about covering the curriculum to jointly examining how they and their students can engage with and talk about content during specific activities and tasks.[6] Our cases suggest that assisting teachers in centering their conversations on student data, including student work samples as well as assessment data, can support these conversations. In addition, explicitly connecting these conversations to lesson planning could be especially helpful to novice teachers because it can assist them in utilizing district and school curricula in ways that help them better understand and foster their students' learning.

Second, the robust development in the disciplinary demand domain that we observed among beginning teachers in the DAI study contrasted with the challenges they experienced with regard to the instructional scaffolding domain. We reported very little change in the novice teachers' instructional scaffolding skills in mathematics or ELA, with the exception of improvement in conceptual strategy instruction in ELA. Given that instructional scaffolding is associated with student learning,[7] it is important for elementary candidates to develop instructional scaffolding skills in mathematics and ELA in courses and clinical placements and to have access to support from instructional coaches once they become full-time teachers. Such assistance should involve helping them acquire content knowledge and pedagogical content knowledge and helping them understand when, how, and why to employ models, strategies, and feedback to support students in addressing ambitious learning objectives.

Currently, methods coursework, especially in elementary mathematics, rarely provides this support.[8] Content-specific methods courses tend to focus on helping elementary candidates learn to engage in unit and lesson planning and about different ways to present content as opposed to helping them learn to teach elementary students conceptual and procedural strategy use, model the use of such strategies, or provide students with feedback.[9] Given that instructional scaffolding, as measured by PLATO, is consistently associated with positive student learning outcomes,[10] preservice preparation programs may be well served to build candidates' foundational knowledge of these practices and to reinforce their utility in clinical support provided by university supervisors. Our data suggest teachers may not naturally develop these practices as they gain teaching experience. As such, they may well need to be reinforced throughout the early years in the classroom. Given that research shows that even experienced teachers struggle to scaffold their students' learning about and use of conceptual and procedural strategies to build their content knowledge, elementary schools would benefit from providing all their teachers support targeted on these practices.

Third, the DAI study helps to illuminate the complex relationship between classroom management and ambitious instruction for beginning teachers. In order to teach ambitiously, teachers must establish behavioral routines and expectations and use class time in ways that support students' engagement in intellectually demanding and meaningful tasks.[11] Yet, being able to manage students' behavior and time effectively will not ensure that beginning teachers develop ambitious instructional practices. Indeed, our findings suggest that we need to consider more carefully the balance between efficient management and ambitious content instruction in beginning teachers' development and how it might shift over time.

In their first and second years of teaching, the teachers we observed for the DAI study had much lower average PLATO scores for the instructional domains than for the classroom environment domain in both mathematics and ELA. At the same time, we also found that candidates who reported more extensive opportunities to learn about, try out, and receive feedback on ambitious mathematics instructional strategies during student teaching had higher PLATO scores in the instructional scaffolding and representations and organization of content instructional domains in mathematics but lower classroom environment scores. Similarly, in their first year of teaching, candidates with higher undergraduate GPAs had higher PLATO scores in the same instructional domains in mathematics and in all three instructional domains in ELA, but lower classroom environment scores in mathematics in their first year of teaching, and lower classroom environment scores in ELA in their second year. These findings suggest that as principals, mentor teachers, and instructional coaches work with and evaluate beginning teachers, helping them to teach more ambitiously might require some trade-offs between encouraging them to engage students in deeper conceptual understanding and efficiently managing their classrooms.

Our findings ultimately suggest that helping novice teachers develop ambitious instructional practices necessitates an expanded notion of classroom management. In particular, ambitious instruction requires that teachers foster students' social and emotional learning, promote positive student relationships, and organize tasks to optimize student learning.[12] It also calls for creating clear classroom rules and anticipating potential challenges.[13] Teacher preparation programs could integrate classroom management and subject matter methods and provide elementary candidates opportunities to practice managing ambitious tasks as they build their understandings of the tasks' conceptual bases.[14] Similarly, principals and instructional coaches could provide novice teachers feedback and support on these dimensions of classroom management and how they are linked with ambitious instruction.

Fourth, our quantitative analyses indicated that beginning teachers who reported having greater opportunities to learn strategies for teaching diverse students had low PLATO mathematics scores in the instructional domains but high PLATO mathematics scores in classroom environment. This suggests that opportunities during teacher preparation to learn about ways to address equity and teach racially, socioeconomically, and linguistically diverse students helped first-year teachers develop relatively strong skills in time and behavior management. But such opportunities did not translate into more rigorous mathematics instruction in the first year. Notably, such learning opportunities during preservice preparation were associated with higher PLATO mathematics scores in instructional scaffolding. Given that teachers in our sample generally struggled to improve in instructional scaffolding between the first and second year, this suggests that opportunities to learn strategies for teaching diverse students had an impact on teachers' instructional scaffolding in mathematics after they had established their time and behavior management skills. This is consistent with qualitative research that has found an apparent impact of preservice preparation over a two-year period after teachers begin full-time teaching.[15]

Fifth, our qualitative analyses suggest that whether preparation learning opportunities matter for beginning teachers' development of more ambitious instructional practices, and how they matter if they do, depends on novices' perceptions and use of them in their work with their students and school colleagues. This has implications for both teacher preparation and elementary schools. Preparation programs need to consider how they engage teacher candidates in making explicit connections between the opportunities to learn ambitious instructional practices they receive in their coursework and their student teaching placements. As our quantitative analyses show, opportunities to learn about and try to enact ambitious instructional practices in student teaching were associated with more ambitious teaching among beginning teachers. The same opportunities offered in methods courses either had no association with more ambitious teaching in mathematics or a negative association in ELA.

At the same time, our case studies showed that having opportunities to learn about and try out practices in both coursework and student teaching can enable novices to deepen their understanding of and skill enacting these practices as beginning teachers. As we documented in chapter 2, the participating preparation programs prepared candidates to enact specific ambitious practices in their student teaching and to reflect on these experiences. In addition, candidates across the programs felt that their programs promoted a shared vision of teaching across their courses and field experiences. Our findings thus point to the continued challenges that teacher educators face in leveraging the opportunities that candidates encounter in student teaching to try out ambitious ELA teaching practices in ways that support similar opportunities in coursework.

Given the limited time candidates spend in any one course, programs might consider being more deliberate in both how they sequence opportunities to learn different ambitious instructional practices across courses and pair these opportunities with school placements in which candidates try the same practices with elementary students. For example, Elham Kazemi and colleagues in mathematics education engaged teacher candidates in rehearsals in which they taught an instructional activity utilizing a specific ambitious instructional practice to their peers in courses and received feedback and coaching from their instructors.[16] Candidates then led the same activity with a group of children, videotaping their teaching for reflection and analysis as part of their methods coursework.

Providing candidates repeated opportunities to investigate, receive feedback, and reflect on their enactment of ambitious practices in and across preparation courses and their work with children assists them in developing their knowledge of when, how, and why to use these practices to support student learning. These types of learning opportunities or enactment pedagogies also provide teacher educators insight into candidates' learning and how to be more responsive to it. They provide a model for how teacher education programs can help candidates make more meaningful connections between their learning in their courses and field placements in ways that build both the conceptual and the practical knowledge they need to teach more ambitiously.

Ultimately, preparation programs may benefit from attending more to how they empower their teacher candidates to utilize the learning opportunities and resources they provide candidates in their student teaching placements and as they transition into their first years of teaching. This would involve working with candidates on how they can navigate relationships with teaching colleagues and also take an active role in directing their own learning and instructional development. While efforts to foster teacher collaboration have been a part of school reform efforts for the past several decades, and mentoring has become a mainstay of beginning teacher induction programs, such efforts do not guarantee either that teachers work closely together or that the support they provide beginning teachers will help novices learn to teach ambitiously.

Teachers' work together can be more or less focused on improving their instruction and the learning opportunities they provide their students. Some beginning teachers in our study felt that in order to teach more ambitiously, they had to separate themselves from their colleagues or, at least, ignore the materials their colleagues shared with them. Others not only learned from their colleagues but also viewed themselves as having valuable knowledge and skills to share with them. Providing candidates opportunities in teacher preparation to build their fluency enacting particular ambitious teaching practices is essential to building the confidence that novice teachers need to navigate collegial relationships in ways that allow them to further cultivate these practices. Preparation programs will also have to help candidates identify different ways in which collegial relationships can support or impede their development so that they can determine whether and how they will take up the guidance their colleagues offer them.

IMPLICATIONS FOR RESEARCH ON TEACHER PREPARATION

The DAI study was a unique study with several important characteristics. It was one of the first studies to collect survey data from elementary teacher candidates from multiple preparation programs about their experiences in courses and their clinical experiences and to follow a large number of them into their first years of full-time teaching. While most large-scale studies of teacher education rely on administrative data and typically focus on student achievement as the central outcome, we collected over one thousand hours of classroom observations, using PLATO, a valid, reliable classroom observation instrument, to analyze the quality of the teachers' mathematics and reading instruction.

Our single-level, multiple linear regression analyses of both survey data and PLATO ratings of beginning teachers' instruction supported inferences about how opportunities to learn in teacher preparation, teacher and school characteristics, and school resources were associated with beginning teachers' enactment of ambitious instruction in mathematics and ELA during their first and second years of teaching. We complemented and extended these inferences with qualitative case studies of a subsample of novice teachers whom we observed and interviewed throughout their first three years of teaching. We recognize, however, that our data prevent us from making definitive claims about causal relationships between such learning opportunities and first- and second-year teachers' enactment of ambitious instruction. Therefore, in this section, we outline a few directions for future research that could test the robustness of our findings.

It is an extremely challenging and time-consuming endeavor for researchers to collect and analyze classroom observation data from graduates of multiple teacher education programs. Nonetheless, one way to strengthen the robustness of the findings reported in this book would be by increasing the number of beginning teachers who participate in classroom observations to at least two hundred. Two developments in recent years provide promising directions for such large-scale research. First, many school districts now rely on video recordings of novice teachers, in addition to or instead of live classroom observations, to assess and provide feedback on the quality of their instruction.

Second, a growing number of researchers have trained neural networks, a form of artificial intelligence, to automatically and accurately identify classroom activity structures and instructional activities in recordings of classroom instruction.[17] As a result, neural networks can now be used to support instructional coaches and principals in providing assistance to first- and second-year teachers and in analyzing video recordings of instruction; that is, they make the process of analyzing instructional quality in videos and providing feedback to novices more efficient. The same neural networks could be used to analyze the ambitiousness of beginning teachers' instruction.

A second way to build on the DAI study would be to design experimental studies that assign elementary teacher candidates at random to treatment and control conditions that enable researchers to make causal inferences about how opportunities to learn in courses and clinical experiences may affect beginning teachers' enactment of ambitious instruction. For example, elementary candidates in the same preparation program would take the same set of courses except that those in the treatment group would take a course in general teaching methods and those in the control group would not take such a course. For another example, elementary candidates in the treatment group would take a course on instructional strategies for diverse students and those in the control group would not take such a course. For a third example, some elementary candidates would be assigned at random to work with a mentor teacher (i.e., a cooperating teacher) who provides them with opportunities to learn about, try out, and receive feedback on efforts to enact ambitious mathematics and ELA instructional strategies, whereas other candidates would be assigned to work with mentor teachers who do not provide such opportunities.

A third way to build on this study would be to carry out small-scale qualitative studies that investigate consistencies and differences across elementary teacher candidates' opportunities to learn ambitious mathematics and ELA strategies in coursework and clinical placements within and across preparation programs. Such studies could explore why candidates in the same program often report varying learning opportunities. They could also consider why, for example, similar opportunities to learn in mathematics and ELA can sometimes lead to differences in novice teachers' enactment of ambitious practice across subject areas.

A fourth way to augment this study would be for researchers to examine the role of instructional coaches in supporting first- and second-year teachers' efforts to teach ambitiously. The DAI study provided evidence that beginning teachers struggle to enact ambitious instruction in mathematics and ELA. Helping them advance their instruction requires that instructional coaches have strong pedagogical content knowledge as well as sufficient time to observe novice teachers and provide them with feedback. Thus, there is a need for research that investigates the consequences of different types of support that coaches provide novice teachers who have varying ability to implement ambitious practices.

CONCLUSION

The instructional practices of elementary teachers in mathematics and English language arts, given the long tail of their potential effects,[18] are important levers for improving student learning in the nation's public schools. In particular, teaching mathematics and ELA ambitiously to elementary students is vitally important. Such instruction can help young children acquire knowledge of core disciplinary concepts and practices and learn to participate in inquiry, reasoning, and argumentation. Students who experience ambitious teaching, in turn, are well positioned to continue learning across content areas and grade levels in school and to thoughtfully interact with other individuals and ideas outside school.

At the same time, ambitious instruction can be challenging for beginning elementary teachers. They must plan for and enact lessons that support students' engagement with mathematical and ELA content in ways that are rigorous, take account of students' identities and learning needs, address student thinking, and promote equitable learning outcomes for historically marginalized students. Teaching ambitiously can be especially demanding for novice elementary teachers who teach multiple subjects and are often in the process of developing effective classroom management skills and building productive relationships with colleagues and parents.

Preservice teacher education has a critical role to play in raising the quality of beginning teachers' instruction. In addition, given the challenges that teaching ambitiously poses for even experienced teachers, elementary schools must also support novice teachers in this work. In this book, we have drawn on findings from our DAI study to identify learning opportunities and resources that can assist beginning teachers in cultivating more ambitious teaching practices. Cross-institutional research, like the DAI study, with data collected from a relatively large number of elementary teacher candidates, can help us to identify effective strategies, including learning opportunities in courses and field experiences, for preparing novice teachers. Such research can also lead to empirically grounded hypotheses that can be tested with larger samples of preparation programs and candidates. Ultimately, designing teacher preparation and induction programs that enable beginning elementary teachers to teach ambitiously will require efforts by teacher educators, school and district leaders, and researchers to work together to ensure that all students have access to instruction that supports their deep conceptual understanding of mathematical and ELA content.

Methodological Appendix

As expectations that beginning teachers teach more ambitiously have increased scrutiny on university-based teacher preparation programs, policy makers and teacher educators alike have called for more robust research that identifies the particular learning-to-teach opportunities that support high-quality teaching across large numbers of preparation program graduates and diverse school contexts.[1] We designed the Development of Ambitious Instruction (DAI) study to respond to this call. Specifically, we used a convergent mixed-methods approach[2] to examine the relationship between novice elementary teachers' individual characteristics, teacher preparation opportunities to learn, and school contexts and resources and their enactment of ambitious instructional practices in mathematics and English language arts (ELA).

Current research typically employs either quantitative methods to examine relationships between features of teacher preparation, such as clinical placement assignments, and teacher effects on student achievement measures or qualitative methods to study how a small number of novice teachers learn to enact a small number of ambitious teaching practices in a particular subject area. In contrast, a convergent mixed-methods approach allows us to utilize both quantitative and qualitative methods to build a more complete understanding of how beginning teachers develop ambitious teaching practices in mathematics and ELA. In this methodological appendix, we first describe the preparation program sample and the beginning teacher sample in the DAI study. Next, we provide details about the survey, classroom observation, and interview measures and protocols that we used and the strategies we employed to analyze them.

TEACHER PREPARATION PROGRAM AND BEGINNING TEACHER SAMPLES

The DAI study followed teacher candidates from five elementary teacher preparation programs from student teaching into their first two to three years of teaching. The five elementary teacher education programs included Cardinal University, Goldfinch University, Meadowlark University, Oriole University, and Robin University (all pseudonyms). In 2015–2016, we collected survey data from final-year elementary teacher candidates at Cardinal, Meadowlark, Oriole, and Robin; in 2016–2017, we collected survey data from final-year elementary teacher candidates at all five programs. These programs collectively prepared approximately 450 to 500 elementary candidates each year in 2015–2016 and 2016–2017. We selected the programs because each incorporated (a) research-based practices and/or (b) practice-based approaches in elementary mathematics and ELA methods courses and because each intentionally organized clinical placements to support candidates' development and enactment of ambitious instruction in mathematics and ELA.

At the same time, the five programs varied in several ways, including characteristics of their universities (e.g., focus, location, and size) and program features, including length of student teaching and structure and sequence of methods courses and field experiences. In chapter 1, we included descriptive information about the programs and how they varied across the sample. For example, four of the programs mandated twelve to fifteen weeks of student teaching, while one required thirty weeks. Three of the programs required two ELA methods courses while two required three courses. Three of the programs required two mathematics methods courses while two required one.

We invited all participating candidates across programs to continue in the study as full-time, first-year elementary teachers. Of the 904 eligible final-year candidates in 2015–2016 and 2016–2017, more than half, or 502 (55.5 percent), completed our Elementary Teacher Candidate survey (see below) and were thus eligible to continue participating in the study. Many of the 502 graduates did not go on to a full-time teaching position; of those who did, eighty-three continued in the study as first-year teachers by participating in classroom observations, surveys, and interviews. Of those eighty-three, sixty-four continued to participate in classroom observations, surveys, and interviews in their second year of teaching.

We also followed thirty of these beginning teachers into their third year of teaching; they continued to participate in classroom observations, surveys, and interviews that year. Of these thirty teachers, we collected intensive case study data (i.e., total of seven interviews and eighteen observations) from sixteen of them. In addition to these teachers, ninety-two additional first-year teachers continued in the study by participating in surveys and interviews (but not classroom observations). Data indicate that the eighty-three teachers in the classroom observations sample of first-year teachers were similar to the other candidates at these universities, suggesting that the findings reported here are generalizable to the total sample of elementary candidates at these five universities.

DATA COLLECTION

Elementary teacher candidate survey

Five hundred two teacher candidates from across the five teacher preparation programs participating in the DAI study completed our Elementary Teacher Candidate survey. This included the eighty-three first-year teachers and sixty-four second-year teachers who participated in classroom observations for the study. All completed our Elementary Teacher Candidate survey during their final year of teacher preparation. This survey addressed elementary candidates' self-reported opportunities to learn about general principles of instruction, strategies for working with diverse students, and ambitious instructional strategies in mathematics and ELA in courses and student teaching. This survey also included items that measured candidates' perceptions of preparation program coherence, their self-efficacy with regard to teaching mathematics and ELA, and a number of covariates such as teacher's race/ethnicity, teacher's gender, and teachers' content knowledge for teaching.

Two items in the Elementary Teacher Candidate survey focused on candidates' opportunities to learn general principles of instruction: "Up to this point in your teacher education program, how much opportunity have you had to learn about general principles and theories of instruction" and about "general methods of teaching (includes lesson planning; motivating students)?" These items were rated on a four-point scale: "none," "touched on it briefly," "spent time discussing or doing it," and "extensive opportunity."

Six items in the Elementary Teacher Candidate survey addressed opportunities to learn strategies for teaching diverse students. These included three items on opportunities to learn about working with specific groups of students: "Up to this point in your teacher education program, how much opportunity have you had to learn about instruction for racially/ethnically diverse students," "linguistically diverse students," and "socioeconomically diverse students?" We also drew on three items that asked about related topics: "In your preparation program, prior to becoming a full-time, certified classroom teacher of record, how much opportunity have you had to gain knowledge about the communities of the students you are likely to teach," "consider the relationship between education and equity," and "develop specific strategies for teaching English language learners (those with limited English proficiency)?" These items were all rated on a four-point scale: "none," "touched on it briefly," "spent time discussing or doing it," and "extensive opportunity."

Twelve items from the Elementary Teacher Candidate survey measured candidates' opportunities to learn ambitious instructional strategies in mathematics and ELA during coursework and their opportunities to learn, try out, and receive feedback on such strategies during their student teaching. These items included designing high levels of cognitive mathematics and ELA tasks for students, teaching strategies for learning mathematics and ELA content, differentiating instruction in mathematics and ELA, connecting mathematics and ELA content to students' prior mathematical and ELA knowledge, connecting mathematics and ELA content to students' personal/cultural experiences, using representations to develop students' mathematical understanding (i.e., using analogies and/or examples to develop students' understanding of ELA concepts), facilitating students' use of technology in doing mathematics (in reading and writing), identifying and responding to common patterns of student thinking in mathematics (i.e., identifying and responding to students' interpretations of ELA texts), facilitating classroom discussion in mathematics and ELA, managing time and student behavior during mathematics and ELA instruction, providing students feedback in learning mathematics and ELA content, and facilitating students' use of manipulatives in doing mathematics.

Elementary teacher candidates were asked to indicate which of the following opportunities they had experienced for each of the ambitious instructional strategy items listed in the previous paragraph: "examined in video or written case," "tried with peers in methods courses," "observed other teachers use this practice with students," "used this practice with students once or twice," "used this practice with students three or more times," "received feedback on my attempts to use this practice with students," or "none of the above."

Six items from the Elementary Teacher Candidate survey measured candidates' perceptions of preparation program coherence. These items included "My program articulates a clear vision of teaching and learning," "I hear similar views about teaching and learning across courses," "What I learn in methods courses reflects what I observe in my field experiences or in my own classroom," "I have gotten to know the other students in my program well," "I feel part of a larger group of people who all share common values with respect to teaching," and "The criteria by which I am evaluated as a student teacher/intern are consistent with what I am taught in my methods courses."

Five items from the Elementary Teacher Candidate survey addressed elementary candidates' self-efficacy related to teaching mathematics and ELA. These items included "Even if I work hard, I will not teach math (ELA) as well as I will most subjects"; "I understand math (ELA) concepts well enough to be effective in teaching math (ELA)"; "I'm not the type to do well in mathematics (ELA)"; "If I work hard, I am confident in my ability to learn new math (ELA) strategies"; and "I have had mostly positive experiences learning mathematics (ELA)."

On the Elementary Teacher Candidate survey, participants reported their gender, race/ethnicity, undergraduate GPA, and SAT/ACT scores; we converted SAT/ACT scores to percentile scores and took steps to equate them.[3] We included each of these covariates in our models.

Content knowledge for teaching surveys

To measure elementary candidates' content knowledge for teaching, we administered two surveys to each candidate. The first survey addressed candidates' Mathematical Knowledge for Teaching,[4] specifically in number and operations, which accounts for 40–50 percent of the US elementary mathematics curriculum.[5] The second survey, known as the survey of Teachers' Knowledge of Reading and Reading Practices, addressed knowledge of how to teach word reading and comprehension.[6] In the analyses presented in this book, we primarily used these two measures as covariates in our quantitative models.

First-year and second-year teacher surveys

The eighty-three first-year teachers who participated in classroom observations for the study all completed our First-Year Teacher survey during their first year of full-time teaching, and sixty-four of them completed our Second-Year Teacher survey in their second year of teaching. The two surveys were almost identical: Both included items that measured the feedback that the beginning teachers received on their use of ambitious instructional strategies in mathematics and ELA from formal mentors, instructional coaches, and principals; their perceptions of fit with their school-based teacher colleagues; their perceptions of collective responsibility at their schools; and their self-efficacy with regard to teaching mathematics and ELA.

These surveys included a question that asked whether participants received feedback on several ambitious mathematics and ELA instructional strategies from mentor teachers, instructional coaches, and principals: "During your two most recent weeks of regular mathematics classroom instruction, how much opportunity did you have to do each of the following?" The list of ambitious strategies was the same as that we used to ask about opportunities to learn in courses and student teaching (see above). The response categories included "Received feedback from my mentor (instructional coach, principal) on my attempts to use this practice with students."

We included a set of items in these surveys that asked about participants' perceptions of the degree to which they fit with their school-based colleagues: Students were asked to indicate their level of agreement or disagreement with each of the following statements: "My approach to teaching mathematics (ELA) fits in with teachers at this school," "My professional interests are the same as those of other teachers throughout this school," "I identify with other teachers throughout this school," "My professional goals are the same as those of other teachers throughout this school," "I matter to other teachers throughout this school," and "Other teachers throughout this school matter to me." Participants were asked to respond on a four-point Likert scale (1–4) indicating the extent to which they agreed with each item. Specifically, higher values in these items indicated agreement.

These surveys featured six items that probed participants' perceptions of the proportion of teachers at their school who shared responsibility for instruction, learning, and behavior. These items included "Help maintain discipline in the entire school, not just their classrooms," "Take responsibility for helping one another do well," "Take responsibility for improving the overall quality of teaching in the school," "Feel responsible for helping students develop self-control," "Set high expectations for academic work," and "Feel responsible for ensuring that all students learn." Participants were asked to respond on a five-point Likert scale with higher values indicating higher proportions of teachers who shared responsibility for instruction, learning, and behavior (i.e., 1 = 0, 2 = less than half of the teachers, 3 = about half, 4 = more than half, 5 = all the teachers).

These surveys measured novice teachers' self-efficacy related to teaching mathematics and ELA in the same way as the Elementary Teacher Candidate survey (see above).

On the First-Year and Second-Year Teacher surveys, participants reported which grade levels they taught. We then converted their responses to either upper elementary (i.e., grades 3–5) or lower elementary (i.e., grades K–2). For first-year teachers and second-year teachers who were working at traditional public schools or charter schools, we drew on the Common Core of Data to include measures of the percentage of students at the teachers' schools who were eligible for free or reduced-price lunch in our models.

Protocol for Language Arts Teaching Observation

In 2016–2017, 2017–2018, and 2018–2019, we observed and video-recorded eighty-three first-year teachers, sixty-four second-year teachers, and thirty third-year teachers teach three mathematics and three ELA lessons each year. For each lesson, we used the Protocol for Language Arts Teaching Observation (PLATO) instrument to assess the ambitiousness of the instruction observed. PLATO includes eleven dimensions of instruction organized in relation to four domains: instructional scaffolding, representations and organization of content, disciplinary demand, and classroom environment.[7] (See chapter 3 for the full list of PLATO's eleven dimensions.) Each element is scored separately on a four-point scale. PLATO also captures teachers' instructional content (e.g., writing, number and operations) and activity structures (e.g., whole group, small group, independent learning). Trained raters scored all the mathematics and ELA lessons, double-scoring 10 percent to assess inter-rater reliability, which resulted in a score of 0.76 in ELA and 0.78 in mathematics. Raters scored each lesson in fifteen-minute segments, rating each PLATO dimension separately on a four-point scale.

PLATO has been used reliably in several studies to assess the relationship between instruction and student achievement gains, and many practices featured in PLATO predict teacher value-added measures.[8] Also, while PLATO was originally developed to measure secondary ELA instruction, Julie Cohen modified it to score mathematics lessons from the Measures of Effective Teaching (MET) study.[9] The main aspects of instruction measured by PLATO (i.e., representations and organization of content, instructional scaffolding, and disciplinary demand) have been a primary focus of recent mathematics education reform efforts in the United States.[10] In modifying PLATO for elementary mathematics, one key change was separating the scale for strategy instruction into two separate scales: one for conceptual strategy instruction and one for procedural strategy instruction.

Beginning teacher interviews

In 2016–2017 and 2017–2018, we conducted three interviews with each of the first-year teachers whom we observed teaching mathematics and ELA. We designed the interviews to understand how beginning teachers forged their instructional practices in and across the subject areas as they (a) interacted with their students, colleagues, and school administrators; (b) made sense of and utilized resources available in their school and district contexts; and (c) drew on the learning opportunities and resources they encountered in their teacher preparation programs. The first interview asked the novices to describe their school, classroom contexts, and students; describe the mathematics and ELA curricula in their schools and districts; explain how they were learning to implement these curricula; identify resources in their schools that helped them teach mathematics and ELA; discuss teacher preparation experiences and resources that helped them teach mathematics and ELA; note challenges that they had experienced; and describe the teacher evaluation process in their schools and districts. We asked about teacher evaluation processes, as evidence suggests that in response to these processes, beginning teachers avoid enacting ambitious teaching practices that present challenges for teachers and students.

The second and third interviews focused specifically on the novices' mathematics and ELA instruction. These interviews asked the beginning teachers to describe their mathematics and ELA instruction; their schools' mathematics and ELA curricula; school expectations for mathematics and ELA instruction; their students' mathematics and ELA learning; district- and school-based resources available to assist them in teaching mathematics and ELA, including materials, guidance, and feedback provided by colleagues, instructional coaches, mentors, and principals; and the teacher preparation learning opportunities and resources they drew on to plan, enact, modify, and improve their mathematics and ELA instruction. These interviews also asked the first-year teachers to identify any changes that occurred in any of the areas we questioned them about.

In 2017–2018 and 2018–2019, we conducted two interviews of the second- and third-year teachers whom we observed teach mathematics and ELA. We used the same protocol that we used in the second and third interviews we conducted with them as first-year teachers (described above). Taken together, the interviews provided insight into the novices' development of their mathematics and ELA instruction and how their beliefs about teaching and learning, teaching self-efficacy, opportunities to learn in their teacher preparation programs, and their school contexts, resources, and interactions shaped this development. We audio-recorded all the interviews and transcribed them for analysis. We also collected and archived all instructional materials that the beginning teachers used during the lessons we observed.

ANALYTIC STRATEGIES

Quantitative analyses

To assess ways in which elementary teacher candidates' learning experiences in teacher preparation were associated with enactment of ambitious instructional practices during the first and second years of teaching, we ran a series of single-level, multiple linear regression analyses. Each regression model tested one of the four PLATO mathematics and ELA domains, the mathematics and ELA instructional composites, or the overall mathematics and ELA composites as the outcome variable. Full information maximum likelihood, or FIML, was used to incorporate cases with missing data on predictor variables, such that the participants included in each analysis predicting a PLATO mathematics outcome included all first- or second-year teachers with PLATO mathematics observational data available, and each analysis predicting a PLATO ELA outcome included all first- or second-year teachers with PLATO ELA observational data available.

In each of the models predicting one of the PLATO instructional domains (i.e., instructional scaffolding, disciplinary demand, and representing content), the classroom environment domain of PLATO was entered as a predictor. Conversely, in the models predicting the PLATO classroom environment domain as the outcome, the PLATO instructional composite score was entered as a predictor, computed as the mean of the three instructional domains. Predictors in each model also included teacher characteristics (i.e., gender, race/ethnicity, undergraduate GPA, SAT/ACT score, teaching self-efficacy) and characteristics of participants' student teaching assignments (i.e., upper versus lower elementary grades, students' socioeconomic status at the school level). Given the sample size of teachers with available observational data, we report findings that reached the $p < .10$ level of significance, in addition to reporting findings at the traditional $p < .05$ level of significance.

To illustrate, the following multiple regression model was used to investigate how teacher preparation opportunities to learn, program coherence, and mathematics teaching self-efficacy were associated with the ambitiousness of beginning teachers' mathematics instruction in the PLATO instructional scaffolding domain. We used similar models to estimate the association between the same independent variables and (a) other individual PLATO mathematics domain scores, (b) individual PLATO ELA domain scores, and (c) PLATO mathematics and ELA composite scores.

The regression model is described below in equation (1):

$$AIMath_{ij} = \beta_{0ij} + \beta_1\, OTLGT_{ij} + \beta_2\, OTLDS_{ij} + \beta_3\, OTLAI_{ij} + \beta_4\, PC_{ij} + \beta_5\, MTSE_{ij} + \beta_6\, P_i + e_t\,, \quad (1)$$

where $AIMath_{ij}$ is the outcome variable (i.e., PLATO mathematics instructional scaffolding scores) for a given beginning teacher i in school j; β_{0ij} is the intercept; $OTLGT_{ij}$ represents the predictor variable opportunities to learn general teaching strategies for teacher i in school j; β_1 captures the conditional association between opportunities to learn general teaching strategies and PLATO mathematics instructional scaffolding scores controlling for all other predictors in the model; $OTLDS_{ij}$ represents the predictor variable opportunities to learn strategies for teaching diverse students for teacher i in school j;

β_2 captures the conditional association between opportunities to learn strategies for teaching diverse students and PLATO mathematics instructional scaffolding scores controlling for all other predictors in the model; $OTLAI_{ij}$ represents the predictor variable opportunities to learn ambitious mathematics instructional strategies for teacher *i* in school *j*; β_3 captures the conditional association between opportunities to learn ambitious mathematics instructional strategies and PLATO mathematics instructional scaffolding scores controlling for all other predictors in the model; and PC_{ij} represents the predictor variable perceived teacher preparation program coherence for teacher *i* in school *j*.

In equation (1), β_4 captures the conditional association between perceived preparation program coherence and PLATO mathematics instructional scaffolding scores controlling for all other predictors in the model; $MTSE_{ij}$ represents the predictor variable mathematics teaching self-efficacy for teacher *i* in school *j*; β_5 captures the conditional association between beginning teachers' mathematics teaching self-efficacy and PLATO mathematics instructional scaffolding scores controlling for all other predictors in the model; P_i represents the set of participant covariates (i.e., gender, race/ethnicity, undergraduate GPA, SAT/ACT score); and β_6 captures the conditional associations between the covariates and PLATO mathematics instructional scaffolding scores controlling for all other predictors in the model. The last term of equation (1)—namely, e_t—is the error term or residual of the outcome.

Qualitative analyses

In chapter 4, we present analyses of interview and observation data that we collected with three beginning teachers during their first three years of teaching. We drew the three cases from a larger sample of sixteen intensive case study teachers whom we followed from teacher preparation into their first three years of teaching. We selected the sixteen teachers based on the relationship between their first-year PLATO mathematics and ELA composite scores and the mean composite scores in each subject of the larger sample of eighty-three first-year teachers. Four of the sixteen teachers had first-year PLATO composite mathematics and ELA scores above the sample composite score means in both subjects (quadrant 1); four had PLATO composite mathematics scores above the sample composite mathematics mean score and PLATO composite ELA scores below the sample composite ELA mean score (quadrant 2); four teachers had PLATO composite mathematics scores below the sample composite mathematics mean score and PLATO composite ELA scores above the sample composite ELA mean scores (quadrant 3); and four teachers had PLATO composite mathematics and ELA scores below the sample mean composite score in both subjects (quadrant 4).

We then iteratively analyzed interview data from the sixteen beginning teachers that we collected during their first, second, and third years of teaching in several phases. In the first stage, we used inductive and thematic coding.[11] This approach enabled us to identify teachers' beliefs about teaching and learning mathematics and ELA; to see how they made sense of, selected, and utilized district- and school-based resources to teach mathematics and ELA; and to understand how they made sense of, selected, and utilized learning opportunities and resources from teacher preparation to teach their mathematics and ELA instruction. We then used cross-case data matrices to identify and compare patterns across beginning teachers' responses based on their PLATO score quadrant. We found that beginning teachers who taught more ambitiously in mathematics and/or ELA tended to report that (a) their districts and schools had clear expectations about mathematics and ELA instruction and provided practical and conceptual resources aligned with these expectations and (b) they themselves employed practical and/or conceptual resources from their teacher preparation programs in their teaching.

We then selected cases, including the three we present in chapter 4, for further analysis to obtain maximum variation across these factors. We further analyzed the three years of interview data for these cases to understand how the cognitive, motivational, and emotional dimensions of the beginning teachers' personal sense shaped and was shaped by their beliefs about teaching and learning and their selection and use of district- and school-based resources and teacher preparation resources and learning opportunities. For each case, we created a case dynamics matrix and wrote analytic memos to identify major themes and patterns within and across the cases.[12]

We took several steps to address credibility and trustworthiness in the qualitative component of this study. At each stage of analysis, two researchers double-coded roughly half the interviews and met to resolve all discrepancies and refine codes before double-coding the remaining interviews. We shared and discussed data matrices and analytic memos to confirm themes and patterns within and across cases and to surface and address disconfirming evidence.[13]

LIMITATIONS

This study had a few limitations. First, our measures of learning opportunities in courses and clinical experiences were based on elementary teacher candidates' self-reports. In other work, we used interview data from teacher education program directors, elementary mathematics methods course instructors, and elementary ELA methods course instructors at four of the universities in our study to provide additional justification for our assertions about candidates' opportunities to learn.[14] Second, teachers, schools, and districts that participated in this study were a volunteer sample; they may have differed from other teachers from the five participating teacher education programs as well as other schools and districts in the states where the beginning teacher study participants taught.

Third, the PLATO observation instrument had previously been used to analyze the quality of ELA and mathematics instruction in upper elementary grades and middle school grades, but it had not previously been used to assess instructional quality in either subject in grades K–2. Also, we were not able to establish causal inference in this study; instead, we sought to identify associations between novice teachers' implementation of ambitious instruction and several factors, including learning opportunities in teacher preparation, using valid and reliable measures of instructional quality. Finally, our findings are potentially subject to omitted variable bias; that is, factors that we were unable to measure may explain some of the variation in beginning teachers' instructional quality.

Notes

Chapter 1

1. Joanne Carlisle, Ben Kelcey, Dan Berebitsky, and Geoffrey Phelps, "Embracing the Complexity of Instruction: A Study of the Effects of Teachers' Instruction on Students' Reading Comprehension," *Scientific Studies of Reading* 15, no. 5 (2011): 409–39; James Hiebert and Douglas A. Grouws, "The Effects of Classroom Mathematics Teaching on Students' Learning," in *Second Handbook of Research on Mathematics Teaching and Learning*, ed. Frank K. Lester Jr. (Information Age, 2007), 371–404; Jihyun Kim, Serena Salloum, Qinyun Lin, and Sihua Hu, "Ambitious Instruction and Student Achievement: Evidence from Early Career Teachers and the TRU Math Observation Instrument," *Teaching and Teacher Education* 117 (2022): 1–12; National Mathematics Advisory Panel, *Foundations for Success: The Final Report of the National Mathematics Advisory Panel* (US Department of Education, 2008); Fred M. Newmann, Anthony S. Bryk, and Jenny K. Nagaoka, *Authentic Intellectual Work and Standardized Tests: Conflict or Coexistence? Improving Chicago's Schools* (Consortium on Chicago School Research, 2001); David Blazar and Casey Archer, "Teaching to Support Students with Diverse Academic Needs," *Educational Researcher* 49, no. 5 (2020): 297–311.
2. Fred Janssen, Pam Grossman, and Hanna Westbroek, "Facilitating Decomposition and Recomposition in Practice-Based Teacher Education: The Power of Modularity," *Teaching and Teacher Education* 51 (2015): 137–46; Matthew A. Kraft and Heather C. Hill, "Developing Ambitious Mathematics Instruction Through Web-Based Coaching: A Randomized Field Trial," *American Educational Research Journal* 57, no. 6 (2020): 2378–2414.
3. Magdalene Lampert and Filippo Graziani, "Instructional Activities as a Tool for Teachers' and Teacher Educators' Learning," *Elementary School Journal* 109, no. 5 (2009): 491–509; Sarah Schneider Kavanagh, Mike Metz, Mary Hauser, Brad Fogo, Megan Westwood Taylor, and Janet Carlson, "Practicing Responsiveness: Using Approximations of Teaching to Develop Teachers' Responsiveness to Students' Ideas," *Journal of Teacher Education* 71, no. 1 (2020): 94–107.
4. Pam Grossman, Sarah Schneider Kavanagh, and Christopher Dean, "The Turn Towards Practice in Teacher Education," in *Teaching Core Practices in Teacher Education*, ed. Pam Grossman (Harvard Education Press, 2022), 1–14.

5. Marilyn Cochran-Smith, "The New Teacher Education: For Better or For Worse?" *Educational Researcher* 34, no. 7 (2005): 3–17; Ken Zeichner, "Rethinking the Connections Between Campus Courses and Field Experiences in College- and University-Based Teacher Education," *Journal of Teacher Education* 61, no. 1–2 (2010): 89–99.
6. Ken Zeichner, "The Struggle for the Soul of Teacher Education in the USA," *Journal of Education for Teaching: International Research and Pedagogy* 40, no. 5 (2014): 551–68.
7. Soheyla Taie and Rebecca Goldring, *Characteristics of Public and Private Elementary and Secondary School Teachers in the United States: Results from the 2017–18 National Teacher and Principal Survey; First Look*, NCES 2020-142 (National Center for Education Statistics, 2020).
8. Raj Chetty, John N. Friedman, and Jonah E. Rockoff, "The Long-Term Impacts of Teachers: Teacher Value-Added and Student Outcomes in Adulthood," Working Paper No. 17699 (National Bureau of Economic Research, 2011).
9. Elham Kazemi, Megan Franke, and Magdalene Lampert, "Developing Pedagogies in Teacher Education to Support Novice Teachers' Ability to Enact Ambitious Instruction," in *Crossing Divides: Proceedings of the 32nd Annual Conference of the Mathematics Education Research Group of Australasia*, vol. 1, ed. R. Hunter, B. Bicknell, and T. Burgess (Palmerston North, New Zealand: Massey University, 2009), 12–30,; Elizabeth A. van Es, Mary Cashen, Tara Barnhart, and Anamarie Auger, "Learning to Notice Mathematics Instruction: Using Video to Develop Preservice Teachers' Vision of Ambitious Pedagogy," *Cognition and Instruction* 35, no. 3 (2017): 165–87.
10. Magdalene Lampert, *Teaching Problems and the Problems of Teaching* (Yale University, 2001); Julia B. Smith, Valerie E. Lee, and Fred M. Newmann, *Instruction and Achievement in Chicago Elementary Schools: Improving Chicago's Schools* (Consortium on Chicago School Research, 2001); Mark Windschitl, Jessica Thompson, Melissa Braaten, and David Stroupe, "Proposing a Core Set of Instructional Practices and Tools for Teachers of Science," *Science Education* 96, no. 5 (2012): 878–903; Eben B. Witherspoon, Nathaniel B. Ferrer, Richard R. Correnti, Mary Kay Stein, and Christian D. Schunn, "Coaching That Supports Teachers' Learning to Enact Ambitious Instruction," *Instructional Science* 49, no. 6 (2021): 877–98.
11. Pam Grossman, Susanna Loeb, Julie Cohen, and James Wyckoff, "Measure for Measure: The Relationship Between Measures of Instructional Practice in Middle School English Language Arts and Teachers' Value-Added Scores," *American Journal of Education* 119, no. 3 (2013): 445–70.
12. Julie Cohen, "Practices That Cross Disciplines? Revisiting Explicit Instruction in Elementary Mathematics and English Language Arts," *Teaching and Teacher Education* 69 (2018): 324–35.

13. Susan B. Empson and Linda Levi, "Extending Children's Mathematics: Fractions and Decimals," *Mathematics Education* 27, no. 4 (2011): 403–34; Mary Kay Stein, Barbara W. Grover, and Marjorie Henningsen, "Building Student Capacity for Mathematical Thinking and Reasoning: An Analysis of Mathematical Tasks Used in Reform Classrooms," *American Educational Research Journal* 33, no. 2 (1996): 455–88.
14. Kazemi et al., "Developing Pedagogies"; Linda Kucan, Annemarie Sullivan Palincsar, Tracy Busse, et al., "Applying the Grossman et al. Theoretical Framework: The Case of Reading," *Teachers College Record* 113, no. 12 (2011): 2897–2921; Magdalene Lampert, Megan Loef Franke, Elham Kazemi, et al., "Keeping It Complex: Using Rehearsals to Support Novice Teacher Learning of Ambitious Teaching," *Journal of Teacher Education* 64, no. 3 (2013): 226–43.
15. Carrie J. Beyer and Elizabeth A. Davis, "Fostering Second Graders' Scientific Explanations: A Beginning Elementary Teacher's Knowledge, Beliefs, and Practice," *Journal of the Learning Sciences* 17, no. 3 (2008): 381–414; Hosun Kang and Mark Windschitl, "How Does Practice-Based Teacher Preparation Influence Novices' First-Year Instruction?" *Teachers College Record* 120, no. 8 (2018): 1–44; Kim et al., "Ambitious Instruction and Student Achievement"; Jessica Thompson, Mark Windschitl, and Melissa Braaten, "Developing a Theory of Ambitious Early-Career Teacher Practice," *American Educational Research Journal* 50, no. 3 (2013): 574–615.
16. Dorothea Anagnostopoulos, Jillian Cavanna, and Sian Charles-Harris, "Managing to Teach Ambitiously in the First Year?" *Elementary School Journal* 120, no. 4 (2020): 667–91; Kang and Windschitl, "Practice-Based Teacher Preparation"; Thompson et al., "Developing a Theory"; Jennifer Y. Kinser-Traut and Erin E. Turner, "Shared Authority in the Mathematics Classroom: Successes and Challenges Throughout One Teacher's Trajectory Implementing Ambitious Practices," *Journal of Mathematics Teacher Education* 23, no. 1 (2020): 5–34; Byungeun Pak, Jillian M. Cavanna, and Brent E. Jackson, "The Relationship Between Number Talks and Ambitious Instruction: Learning from Beginning Teachers," *Mathematical Thinking and Learning* (2023): 1–24; David Stroupe, "Beginning Teachers' Use of Resources to Enact and Learn from Ambitious Instruction," *Cognition and Instruction* 34, no. 1 (2016): 51–77.
17. Thompson et al., "Developing a Theory."
18. Donald J. Boyd, Pamela L. Grossman, Hamilton Lankford, Susanna Loeb, and James Wyckoff, "Teacher Preparation and Student Achievement," *Educational Evaluation and Policy Analysis* 31, no. 4 (2009): 416–40.
19. Matthew Ronfeldt, "Field Placement Schools and Instructional Effectiveness," *Journal of Teacher Education* 66, no. 4 (2015): 304–20; Matthew Ronfeldt, Stacey L. Brockman, and Shanyce L. Campbell, "Does Cooperating Teachers' Instructional Effectiveness Improve Preservice Teachers' Future Performance?" *Educational Researcher* 47, no. 7 (2018): 405–18; Dan Goldhaber, John M. Krieg,

and Roddy Theobald, "Does the Match Matter? Exploring Whether Student Teaching Experiences Affect Teacher Effectiveness," *American Educational Research Journal* 54, no. 2 (2017): 325–59.

20. Boyd et al., "Teacher Preparation and Student Achievement"; Dan Goldhaber, Stephanie Liddle, and Roddy Theobald, "The Gateway to the Profession: Assessing Teacher Preparation Programs Based on Student Achievement," *Economics of Education Review* 34 (2013): 29–44; Cory Koedel, Eric Parsons, Michael Podgursky, and Mark Ehlert, "Teacher Preparation Programs and Teacher Quality: Are There Real Differences Across Programs?" *Education Finance and Policy* 10, no. 4 (2015): 508–34; Kata Mihaly, Daniel McCaffrey, Tim R. Sass, and J. R. Lockwood, "Where You Come From or Where You Go? Distinguishing Between School Quality and the Effectiveness of Teacher Preparation Program Graduates," *Education Finance and Policy* 8, no. 4 (2013): 459–93.
21. Dan C. Lortie, *Schoolteacher: A Sociological Study* (University of Chicago Press, 2020).
22. Grossman et al., "Measure for Measure."
23. Pam Grossman, Julie Cohen, Matthew Ronfeldt, and Lindsay Brown, "The Test Matters: The Relationship Between Classroom Observation Scores and Teacher Value Added on Multiple Types of Assessment," *Educational Researcher* 43, no. 6 (2014): 293–303; Thomas J. Kane and Douglas O. Staiger, *Gathering Feedback for Teaching: Combining High-Quality Observations with Student Surveys and Achievement Gains*, MET Project research paper (Bill & Melinda Gates Foundation, 2012).
24. Julie Cohen, "Challenges in Identifying High-Leverage Practices," *Teachers College Record* 117, no. 7 (2015): 1–41; Cohen, "Practices That Cross Disciplines?"; Julie Cohen, Lorien Chambers Schuldt, Lindsay Brown, and Pam Grossman, "Leveraging Observation Tools for Instructional Improvement: Exploring Variability in Uptake of Ambitious Instructional Practices," *Teachers College Record* 118, no. 11 (2016): 1–36; The MET study, funded by the Bill & Melinda Gates Foundation, analyzed thirteen thousand lessons from three thousand teachers in seven urban school districts in the United States to test new approaches to identifying effective teaching. Bill & Melinda Gates Foundation, *Learning About Teaching: Findings from the Measures for Effective Teaching Project*, 2010, retrieved from https://cepr.harvard.edu/sites/hwpi.harvard.edu/files/cepr/files/met-brief-learning-about-teaching.pdf.
25. DeAnn Huinker, Cathery Yeh, and Anne Marie Marshall, *Catalyzing Change in Early Childhood and Elementary Mathematics: Initiating Critical Conversations* (National Council of Teachers of Mathematics, 2020); Steve Leinwand, *Principles to Actions: Ensuring Mathematical Success for All* (National Council of Teachers of Mathematics, 2014).
26. Taie and Goldring, *Characteristics.*

Chapter 2

1. David Stroupe, Karen Hammerness, and Scott McDonald, "Practice-Based Science Teacher Education," in *Preparing Science Teachers Through Practice-Based Teacher Education*, ed. David Stroupe, Karen Hammerness, and Scott McDonald (Harvard Education Press, 2020), 1–12.
2. Fred Korthagen, "Inconvenient Truths About Teacher Learning: Towards Professional Development 3.0," *Teachers and Teaching* 23, no. 4 (2017): 387–405.
3. Lauren M. Anderson and Jamy A. Stillman, "Student Teaching's Contribution to Preservice Teacher Development: A Review of Research Focused on the Preparation of Teachers for Urban and High-Needs Contexts," *Review of Educational Research* 83, no. 1 (2013): 3–69.
4. Linda Darling-Hammond and John Bransford, eds., *Preparing Teachers for a Changing World: What Teachers Should Learn and Be Able to Do* (Wiley, 2007); Morva A. McDonald, "The Integration of Social Justice in Teacher Education: Dimensions of Prospective Teachers' Opportunities to Learn," *Journal of Teacher Education* 56, no. 5 (2005): 418–35.
5. Thomas H. Levine, Glenn Tatsuya Mitoma, Dorothea M. Anagnostopoulos, and Rene Roselle, "Exploring the Nature, Facilitators, and Challenges of Program Coherence in a Case of Teacher Education Program Redesign Using Core Practices," *Journal of Teacher Education* 74, no. 1 (2023): 69–84.
6. Chandra L. Alston, Katie A. Danielson, Elizabeth Dutro, and Ashley Cartun, "Does a Discussion by Any Other Name Sound the Same? Teaching Discussion in Three ELA Methods Courses," *Journal of Teacher Education* 69, no. 3 (2018): 225–38; Julie Cohen and Rebekah Berlin, "What Constitutes an 'Opportunity to Learn' in Teacher Preparation?" *Journal of Teacher Education* 71, no. 4 (2020): 434–48; Elizabeth A. Davis, Matthew Kloser, Andrea Wells, Mark Windschitl, Janet Carlson, and John-Carlos Marino, "Teaching the Practice of Leading Sense-Making Discussions in Science: Science Teacher Educators Using Rehearsals," *Journal of Science Teacher Education* 28, no. 3 (2017): 275–93; Hosun Kang and Mark Windschitl, "How Does Practice-Based Teacher Preparation Influence Novices' First-Year Instruction?" *Teachers College Record* 120, no. 8 (2018): 1–44.
7. Cohen and Berlin, "What Constitutes an 'Opportunity to Learn'?"
8. William H. Schmidt, Leland Cogan, and Richard Houang, "The Role of Opportunity to Learn in Teacher Preparation: An International Context," *Journal of Teacher Education* 62, no. 2 (2011): 138–53, see esp. 140.
9. William H. Schmidt, Richard T. Houang, Leland Cogan, et al., "Opportunity to Learn in the Preparation of Mathematics Teachers: Its Structure and How It Varies Across Six Countries," *ZDM, International Journal of Mathematics Education* 40 (2008): 735–47.
10. Donald J. Boyd, Pamela L. Grossman, Hamilton Lankford, Susanna Loeb, and James Wyckoff, "Teacher Preparation and Student Achievement," *Educational Evaluation and Policy Analysis* 31, no. 4 (2009): 416–40.

11. Pam Grossman, ed., *Teaching Core Practices in Teacher Education* (Harvard Education Press, 2021).
12. Pam Grossman, "Framework for Teaching Practice: A Brief History of an Idea," *Teachers College Record* 113, no. 12 (2011): 2836–43; Pam Grossman and Morva McDonald, "Back to the Future: Directions for Research in Teaching and Teacher Education," *American Educational Research Journal* 45, no. 1 (2008): 184–205; Fred Janssen, Pam Grossman, and Hanna Westbroek, "Facilitating Decomposition and Recomposition in Practice-Based Teacher Education: The Power of Modularity," *Teaching and Teacher Education* 51 (2015): 137–46; Morva McDonald, Elham Kazemi, and Sarah Schneider Kavanagh, "Core Practices and Pedagogies of Teacher Education: A Call for a Common Language and Collective Activity," *Journal of Teacher Education* 64, no. 5 (2013): 378–86.
13. Kang and Windschitl, "Practice-Based Teacher Preparation Influence"; David Stroupe, "Beginning Teachers' Use of Resources to Enact and Learn from Ambitious Instruction," *Cognition and Instruction* 34, no. 1 (2016): 51–77; Jessica Thompson, Mark Windschitl, and Melissa Braaten, "Developing a Theory of Ambitious Early-Career Teacher Practice," *American Educational Research Journal* 50, no. 3 (2013): 574–615.
14. Jessica Thompson, Kirsten Mawyer, Heather Johnson, Deana Scipio, and April Luehmann, "Culturally and Linguistically Sustaining Approaches to Ambitious Science Teaching Pedagogies," in *Preparing Science Teachers Through Practice-Based Teacher Education*, ed. David Stroupe, Karen Hammerness, and Scott McDonald (Harvard Education Press, 2020), 45–61.
15. Angela Calabrese Barton, Edna Tan, and Daniel J. Birmingham, "Rethinking High-Leverage Practices in Justice-Oriented Ways," *Journal of Teacher Education* 71, no. 4 (2020): 477–94, see esp. 479.
16. Thompson et al., "Culturally and Linguistically Sustaining Approaches."
17. Linda Darling-Hammond, "Constructing 21st-Century Teacher Education," *Journal of Teacher Education* 57, no. 3 (2006): 300–14; Pam Grossman, Karen M. Hammerness, Morva McDonald, and Matt Ronfeldt, "Constructing Coherence: Structural Predictors of Perceptions of Coherence in NYC Teacher Education Programs," *Journal of Teacher Education* 59, no. 4 (2008): 273–87; Karen Hammerness and Kirsti Klette, "Indicators of Quality in Teacher Education: Looking at Features of Teacher Education from an International Perspective," in *Promoting and Sustaining a Quality Teacher Workforce*, vol. 27, ed. Alexander W. Wiseman and Gerald K. LeTendre (Emerald Group, 2015), 239–77; Maria Teresa Tatto, "Examining Values and Beliefs About Teaching Diverse Students: Understanding the Challenges for Teacher Education," *Educational Evaluation and Policy Analysis* 18, no. 2 (1996): 155–80; Karen Moore Hammerness, "A Comparative Study of Three Key Features in the Design and Practice of Teacher

Education in the United States and Norway: Part I. Findings from a Study in the United States [VISIONS 2011: Teacher Education]," *Acta Didactica Norge* 6, no. 1 (2012): Art. 18.

18. Hammerness and Klette, "Quality in Teacher Education."
19. Sharon Feiman-Nemser, Eran Tamir, and Karen Hammerness, eds., *Inspiring Teaching: Preparing Teachers to Succeed in Mission-Driven Schools* (Harvard Education Press, 2014).
20. Feiman-Nemser et al., *Inspiring Teaching.*
21. Sigrid Blömeke, Lynn Paine, Richard T. Houang, et al., "Future Teachers' Competence to Plan a Lesson: First Results of a Six-Country Study on the Efficiency of Teacher Education," *ZDM, International Journal on Mathematics Education* 40 (2008): 749–62; Johannes König, Sigrid Blömeke, Lynn Paine, William H. Schmidt, and Feng-Jui Hsieh, "General Pedagogical Knowledge of Future Middle School Teachers: On the Complex Ecology of Teacher Education in the United States, Germany, and Taiwan," *Journal of Teacher Education* 62, no. 2 (2011): 188–201.
22. David Blazar, "Effective Teaching in Elementary Mathematics: Identifying Classroom Practices That Support Student Achievement," *Economics of Education Review* 48 (2015): 16–29; Julie Cohen, Erik Ruzek, and Lia Sandilos, "Does Teaching Quality Cross Subjects? Exploring Consistency in Elementary Teacher Practice Across Subjects," *AERA Open* 4, no. 3 (2018): 2332858418794492; Pam Grossman, Susanna Loeb, Julie Cohen, and James Wyckoff, "Measure for Measure: The Relationship Between Measures of Instructional Practice in Middle School English Language Arts and Teachers' Value-Added Scores," *American Journal of Education* 119, no. 3 (2013): 445–70; Thompson et al., "Developing a Theory," 229–51.
23. Gloria Ladson-Billings, "Culturally Relevant Pedagogy 2.0: Aka the Remix," *Harvard Educational Review* 84, no. 1 (2014): 74–84; Django Paris and H. Samy Alim, "What Are We Seeking to Sustain Through Culturally Sustaining Pedagogy? A Loving Critique Forward," *Harvard Educational Review* 84, no. 1 (2014): 85–100.
24. Motoko Akiba, "Identifying Program Characteristics for Preparing Pre-Service Teachers for Diversity," *Teachers College Record* 113, no. 3 (2011): 658–97; Revathy Kumar and Fani Lauermann, "Cultural Beliefs and Instructional Intentions: Do Experiences in Teacher Education Institutions Matter?" *American Educational Research Journal* 55, no. 3 (2018): 419–52; Kamau Oginga Siwatu, "Preservice Teachers' Culturally Responsive Teaching Self-Efficacy–Forming Experiences: A Mixed Methods Study," *Journal of Educational Research* 104, no. 5 (2011): 360–69.
25. Feiman-Nemser et al., *Inspiring Teaching*; Mary M. Kennedy, *Learning to Teach Writing: Does Teacher Education Make a Difference?* (Teachers College Press, 1998).

Chapter 3

1. Raj Chetty, John N. Friedman, and Jonah E. Rockoff, "The Long-Term Impacts of Teachers: Teacher Value-Added and Student Outcomes in Adulthood," Working Paper No. 17699 (National Bureau of Economic Research, 2011); Task Group on Teacher Quality, Steven Glazerman, Susanna Loeb, Daniel D. Goldhaber, Stephen Raudenbush, and Grover J. Whitehurst, *Evaluating Teachers: The Important Role of Value-Added* (Brookings Brown Center on Education Policy, 2010), https://www.brookings.edu/articles/evaluating-teachers-the-important-role-of-value-added/; Andrew J. Wayne and Peter Youngs, "Teacher Characteristics and Student Achievement Gains: A Review," *Review of Educational Research* 73, no. 1 (2003): 89–122.
2. David Stroupe, Amelia Gotwals, Julie Christensen, and Kraig A. Wray, "Becoming Ambitious: How a Practice-Based Methods Course and 'Macroteaching' Shaped Beginning Teachers' Critical Pedagogical Discourses," *Journal of Science Teacher Education* 33, no. 6 (2022): 683–702.
3. Sarah Schneider Kavanagh, Jenni Conrad, and Sarah Dagogo-Jack, "From Rote to Reasoned: Examining the Role of Pedagogical Reasoning in Practice-Based Teacher Education," *Teaching and Teacher Education* 89, no. 4 (2020).
4. Donald Boyd, Hamilton Lankford, Susanna Loeb, Jonah Rockoff, and James Wyckoff, "The Narrowing Gap in New York City Teacher Qualifications and Its Implications for Student Achievement in High-Poverty Schools," Working Paper No. 14021 (National Bureau of Economic Research, 2008); Charles T. Clotfelter, Helen F. Ladd, and Jacob L. Vigdor, "Teacher Credentials and Student Achievement: Longitudinal Analysis with Student Fixed Effects," *Economics of Education Review* 26, no. 6 (2007): 673–82; John P. Papay and Matthew A. Kraft, "Productivity Returns to Experience in the Teacher Labor Market: Methodological Challenges and New Evidence on Long-Term Career Improvement," *Journal of Public Economics* 130 (2015): 105–19.
5. Pam Grossman, Susanna Loeb, Julie Cohen, and James Wyckoff, "Measure for Measure: The Relationship Between Measures of Instructional Practice in Middle School English Language Arts and Teachers' Value-Added Scores," *American Journal of Education* 119, no. 3 (2013): 445–70.
6. Julie Cohen, "Challenges in Identifying High-Leverage Practices," *Teachers College Record* 117, no. 7 (2015): 1–41.
7. DeAnn Huinker, Cathery Yeh, and Anne Marie Marshall, *Catalyzing Change in Early Childhood and Elementary Mathematics: Initiating Critical Conversations* (National Council of Teachers of Mathematics, 2020); Steve Leinwand, *Principles to Actions: Ensuring Mathematical Success for All* (National Council of Teachers of Mathematics, 2014).
8. Heather Hill and Pam Grossman, "Learning from Teacher Observations: Challenges and Opportunities Posed by New Teacher Evaluation Systems," *Harvard Educational Review* 83, no. 2 (2013): 371–84.

9. We present results in both raw scores and Cohen's *d* effect size, calculated using the year 1 sample standard deviation for a given subject, domain, and/or dimension.
10. Pam Grossman, Julie Cohen, and Lindsay Brown, "Understanding Instructional Quality in English Language Arts: Variations in PLATO Scores by Content and Context," in *Designing Teacher Evaluation Systems: New Guidance from the Measures of Effective Teaching Project*, ed. Thomas J. Kane, Kerri A. Kerr, and Robert Pianta (Jossey-Bass, 2014), 303–31.
11. Cohen, "Challenges."
12. Pam Grossman and Clarissa Thompson, "Learning from Curriculum Materials: Scaffolds for New Teachers?" *Teaching and Teacher Education* 24, no. 8 (2008): 2014–26; David Kauffman, Susan Moore Johnson, Susan M. Kardos, Edward Liu, and Heather G. Peske, "'Lost at Sea': New Teachers' Experiences with Curriculum and Assessment," *Teachers College Record* 104, no. 2 (2002): 273–300.
13. Lindsay Clare Matsumura, Helen E. Garnier, and Jessaca Spybrook, "The Effect of Content-Focused Coaching on the Quality of Classroom Text Discussions," *Journal of Teacher Education* 63, no. 3 (2012): 214–28; Randi Nevins Stanulis, Sarah Little, and Erin Wibbens, "Intensive Mentoring That Contributes to Change in Beginning Elementary Teachers' Learning to Lead Classroom Discussions," *Teaching and Teacher Education* 28, no. 1 (2012): 32–43.
14. Timothy Boerst, Laurie Sleep, Deborah Ball, and Hyman Bass, "Preparing Teachers to Lead Mathematics Discussions," *Teachers College Record* 113, no. 12 (2011): 2844–77; Hala Ghousseini, "Core Practices and Problems of Practice in Learning to Lead Classroom Discussions," *Elementary School Journal* 115, no. 3 (2015): 334–57; Linda Kucan, Annemarie Sullivan Palincsar, Tracy Busse, et al., "Applying the Grossman et al. Theoretical Framework: The Case of Reading," *Teachers College Record* 113, no. 12 (2011): 2897–2921.
15. Cohen, "Challenges"; Thomas J. Kane and Douglas O. Staiger, *Gathering Feedback for Teaching: Combining High-Quality Observations with Student Surveys and Achievement Gains*, MET Project research paper (Bill & Melinda Gates Foundation, 2012).
16. The material in this section originally appeared in *Teaching and Teacher Education*, volume 110. Peter Youngs, Lauren Molloy Elreda, Dorothea Anagnostopoulos, Julie Cohen, Corey Drake, and Spyros Konstantopoulos, "The Development of Ambitious Instruction: How Beginning Elementary Teachers' Preparation Experiences Are Associated with Their Mathematics and English Language Arts Instructional Practices," *Teaching and Teacher Education* 110 (Elsevier, 2022), 1–14.
17. These categories were first conceptualized by Pam Grossman and her colleagues in Pam Grossman, Christa Compton, Danielle Igra, Matthew Ronfeldt, Emily Shahan, and Peter W. Williamson, "Teaching Practice: A Cross-Professional Perspective," *Teachers College Record* 111, no. 9 (2009): 2055–2100; see also

Hosun Kang and Mark Windschitl, "How Does Practice-Based Teacher Preparation Influence Novices' First-Year Instruction?" *Teachers College Record* 120, no. 8 (2018): 1–44; Melinda M. Leko and Mary T. Brownell, "Special Education Preservice Teachers' Appropriation of Pedagogical Tools for Teaching Reading," *Exceptional Children* 77, no. 2 (2011): 229–51; David Stroupe, "Beginning Teachers' Use of Resources to Enact and Learn from Ambitious Instruction," *Cognition and Instruction* 34, no. 1 (2016): 51–77; David Stroupe, Karen Hammerness, and Scott McDonald, eds., *Preparing Science Teachers Through Practice-Based Teacher Education* (Harvard Education Press, 2020); Jessica Thompson, Mark Windschitl, and Melissa Braaten, "Developing a Theory of Ambitious Early-Career Teacher Practice," *American Educational Research Journal* 50, no. 3 (2013): 574–615.

18. Matthew Ronfeldt, "Where Should Student Teachers Learn to Teach? Effects of Field Placement School Characteristics on Teacher Retention and Effectiveness," *Educational Evaluation and Policy Analysis* 34, no. 1 (2012): 3–26; Matthew Ronfeldt, "Field Placement Schools and Instructional Effectiveness," *Journal of Teacher Education* 66, no. 4 (2015): 304–20; Matthew Ronfeldt, Kavita Kapadia Matsko, Hillary Greene Nolan, and Michelle Reininger, "Three Different Measures of Graduates' Instructional Readiness and the Features of Preservice Preparation That Predict Them," *Journal of Teacher Education* 72, no. 1 (2021): 56–71.
19. Sigrid Blömeke, Lynn Paine, Richard T. Houang, et al., "Future Teachers' Competence to Plan a Lesson: First Results of a Six-Country Study on the Efficiency of Teacher Education," *ZDM, International Journal of Mathematics Education* 40 (2008): 749–62; Johannes König, Sigrid Blömeke, Lynn Paine, William H. Schmidt, and Feng-Jui Hsieh, "General Pedagogical Knowledge of Future Middle School Teachers: On the Complex Ecology of Teacher Education in the United States, Germany, and Taiwan," *Journal of Teacher Education* 62, no. 2 (2011): 188–201; Lee Shulman, "Knowledge and Teaching: Foundations of the New Reform," *Harvard Educational Review* 57, no. 1 (1987): 1–23.
20. Donald J. Boyd, Pamela L. Grossman, Hamilton Lankford, Susanna Loeb, and James Wyckoff, "Teacher Preparation and Student Achievement," *Educational Evaluation and Policy Analysis* 31, no. 4 (2009): 416–40; Peter Youngs and Hong Qian, "The Influence of University Courses and Field Experiences on Chinese Elementary Candidates' Mathematical Knowledge for Teaching," *Journal of Teacher Education* 64, no. 3 (2013): 244–61.
21. Geneva Gay, "Preparing for Culturally Responsive Teaching," *Journal of Teacher Education* 53, no. 2 (2002): 106–16; Gloria Ladson-Billings, "Toward a Theory of Culturally Relevant Pedagogy," *American Educational Research Journal* 32, no. 3 (1995): 465–91; Django Paris and H. Samy Alim, "What Are We Seeking to Sustain Through Culturally Sustaining Pedagogy? A Loving Critique Forward," *Harvard Educational Review* 84, no. 1 (2014): 85–100.

22. Magdalene Lampert and Filippo Graziani, "Instructional Activities as a Tool for Teachers' and Teacher Educators' Learning," *Elementary School Journal* 109, no. 5 (2009): 491–509.
23. See, e.g., Susan Chambers Cantrell and Hannah K. Hughes, "Teacher Efficacy and Content Literacy Implementation: An Exploration of the Effects of Extended Professional Development with Coaching," *Journal of Literacy Research* 40, no. 1 (2008): 95–127; Heather C. Hill, Merrie L. Blunk, Charalambos Y. Charalambous, et al., "Mathematical Knowledge for Teaching and the Mathematical Quality of Instruction: An Exploratory Study," *Cognition and Instruction* 26, no. 4 (2008): 430–511.
24. See, e.g., Heather C. Hill, Brian Rowan, and Deborah Loewenberg Ball, "Effects of Teachers' Mathematical Knowledge for Teaching on Student Achievement," *American Educational Research Journal* 42, no. 2 (2005): 371–406; Anita Woolfolk Hoy and Heather A. Davis, "Teacher Self-Efficacy and Its Influence on the Achievement of Adolescents," in *Self-Efficacy Beliefs of Adolescents*, ed. Frank Pajeres and Tim Urdan (Information Age, 2006), 117–38.
25. Grossman et al., "Understanding Instructional Quality."
26. Blömeke et al., "Future Teachers' Competence"; König et al., "General Pedagogical Knowledge"; Shulman, "Knowledge and Teaching."
27. Kavita Kapadia Matsko, Matthew Ronfeldt, Hillary Greene Nolan, Joshua Klugman, Michelle Reininger, and Stacey L. Brockman, "Cooperating Teacher as Model and Coach: What Leads to Student Teachers' Perceptions of Preparedness?" *Journal of Teacher Education* 71, no. 1 (2020): 41–62; M. Ronfeldt, *Links Among Teacher Preparation, Retention, and Teaching Effectiveness: Evaluating and Improving Teacher Preparation Programs* (National Academy of Education, 2021).
28. Jennifer Y. Kinser-Traut and Erin E. Turner, "Shared Authority in the Mathematics Classroom: Successes and Challenges Throughout One Teacher's Trajectory Implementing Ambitious Practices," *Journal of Mathematics Teacher Education* 23, no. 1 (2020): 5–34; Annela Teemant, Joan Wink, and Serena Tyra, "Effects of Coaching on Teacher Use of Sociocultural Instructional Practices," *Teaching and Teacher Education* 27, no. 4 (2011): 683–93.
29. Angela Calabrese Barton, Edna Tan, and Daniel J. Birmingham, "Rethinking High-Leverage Practices in Justice-Oriented Ways," *Journal of Teacher Education* 71, no. 4 (2020): 477–94; Thompson, Windschitl, and Braaten, "Developing a Theory."
30. Matsko et al., "Cooperating Teacher"; Ronfeldt, *Links*.
31. Linda Darling-Hammond, "Constructing 21st-Century Teacher Education," *Journal of Teacher Education* 57, no. 3 (2006): 300–314; Pam Grossman, Karen M. Hammerness, Morva McDonald, and Matt Ronfeldt, "Constructing Coherence: Structural Predictors of Perceptions of Coherence in NYC Teacher Education Programs," *Journal of Teacher Education* 59, no. 4 (2008): 273–87; Karen Hammerness and Kirsti Klette, "Indicators of Quality in Teacher Education:

Looking at Features of Teacher Education from an International Perspective," in *Promoting and Sustaining a Quality Teacher Workforce*, vol. 27, ed. Alexander W. Wiseman and Gerald K. LeTendre (Emerald Group, 2015), 239–77; Maria Teresa Tatto, "Examining Values and Beliefs About Teaching Diverse Students: Understanding the Challenges for Teacher Education," *Educational Evaluation and Policy Analysis* 18, no. 2 (1996): 155–80; Karen Moore Hammerness, "A Comparative Study of Three Key Features in the Design and Practice of Teacher Education in the United States and Norway: Part I. Findings from a Study in the United States [VISIONS 2011: Teacher Education]," *Acta Didactica Norge* 6, no. 1 (2012): Art. 18.

Chapter 4

1. Pam Grossman and Clarissa Thompson, "Learning from Curriculum Materials: Scaffolds for New Teachers?" *Teaching and Teacher Education* 24, no. 8 (2008): 2014–26; David Stroupe, "Beginning Teachers' Use of Resources to Enact and Learn from Ambitious Instruction," *Cognition and Instruction* 34, no. 1 (2016): 51–77.
2. Pamela L. Grossman, Peter Smagorinsky, and Sheila Valencia, "Appropriating Tools for Teaching English: A Theoretical Framework for Research on Learning to Teach," *American Journal of Education* 108, no. 1 (1999): 1–29; Hosun Kang and Mark Windschitl, "How Does Practice-Based Teacher Preparation Influence Novices' First-Year Instruction?" *Teachers College Record* 120, no. 8 (2018): 1–44.
3. Pam Grossman, Sarah Schneider Kavanagh, and Christopher Dean, "The Turn Towards Practice in Teacher Education," in *Teaching Core Practices in Teacher Education*, ed. Pam Grossman (Harvard Education Press, 2022), 1–14; Dan C. Lortie, *Schoolteacher: A Sociological Study* (University of Chicago Press, 2020).
4. Korthagen argues that teacher learning largely occurs unconsciously and involves cognitive, emotional, and motivational dimensions. See Fred Korthagen, "Inconvenient Truths About Teacher Learning: Towards Professional Development 3.0," *Teachers and Teaching* 23, no. 4 (2017): 387–405. The concept of personal sense, which we draw from cultural historical activity theory, similarly focuses on these dimensions of learning. It expands the focus of much research on teacher learning that employs cultural-historical activity theory to more fully recognize the subjective, individual dimension of teaching learning while also recognizing its socially situated nature. See Anna Stetsenko and Igor M. Arievitch, "The Self in Cultural-Historical Activity Theory: Reclaiming the Unity of Social and Individual Dimensions of Human Development," *Theory & Psychology* 14, no. 4 (2004): 475–503.
5. Our notion of social resources extends to the notions of conceptual and practical resources that we draw from the work of Pamela Grossman, Peter Smagorinsky, and Sheila Valencia. See Grossman et al., "Appropriating Tools for Teaching English."

6. Byungeun Pak and Corey Drake, "Tracing Beginning Teachers' Mathematics Curriculum Use in Their First Three Years of Teaching," in *Proceedings of the Forty-Third Annual Meeting of the North American Chapter of the International Group for the Psychology of Mathematics Education* (Philadelphia, 2021); Sheila W. Valencia, Nancy A. Place, Susan D. Martin, and Pamela L. Grossman, "Curriculum Materials for Elementary Reading: Shackles and Scaffolds for Four Beginning Teachers," *Elementary School Journal* 107, no. 1 (2006): 93–120.
7. Janine T. Remillard, Beth A. Herbel-Eisenmann, and Gwendolyn M. Lloyd, *Mathematics Teachers at Work* (Routledge, 2009).
8. See B. S. Bratus, "Personal Sense According to A. N. Leontiev and the Problem of a Vertical Axis of Consciousness," *Journal of Russian & East European Psychology* 43, no. 6 (2005): 32–44; Jeanette A. Lawrence and Jaan Valsiner, "Making Personal Sense: An Account of Basic Internalization and Externalization Processes," *Theory & Psychology* 13, no. 6 (2003): 723–52; Alekseĭ Nikolaevich Leont'ev, *Activity, Consciousness, and Personality*, trans. M. J. Hall (Prentice-Hall, 1978); Anna Stetsenko, "Activity as Object-Related: Resolving the Dichotomy of Individual and Collective Planes of Activity," *Mind, Culture, and Activity* 12, no. 1 (2005): 70–88.
9. Julie Cohen, "Challenges in Identifying High-Leverage Practices," *Teachers College Record* 117, no. 7 (2015): 1–41; Julie Cohen, "Practices That Cross Disciplines? Revisiting Explicit Instruction in Elementary Mathematics and English Language Arts," *Teaching and Teacher Education* 69 (2018): 324–35; Julie Cohen, Lorien Chambers Schuldt, Lindsay Brown, and Pam Grossman, "Leveraging Observation Tools for Instructional Improvement: Exploring Variability in Uptake of Ambitious Instructional Practices," *Teachers College Record* 118, no. 11 (2016).
10. We use the term *district curriculum* to refer to the scope and sequence of content, assessment, and instructional units that districts delineate to guide and sometimes mandate what teachers should teach, how, and at what point in the school year. These documents, which include pacing guides, can delineate content, learning goals, instructional approaches, assessments, and timelines. We use the term *curriculum program* to refer to those curricular packages that districts purchase and that include materials such as textbooks, teachers' guides, and digital resources. District curricula can be centered around curriculum programs but go beyond them in guiding how teachers can or are expected to use curriculum programs.
11. Deborah Loewenberg Ball and Francesca M. Forzani, "The Work of Teaching and the Challenge for Teacher Education," *Journal of Teacher Education* 60, no. 5 (2009): 497–511; Pam Grossman, Karen Hammerness, and Morva McDonald, "Redefining Teaching, Re-Imagining Teacher Education," *Teachers and Teaching: Theory and Practice* 15, no. 2 (2009): 273–89; Magdalene Lampert, "Learning Teaching in, from, and for Practice: What Do We Mean?" *Journal of Teacher Education* 61, no. 1–2 (2010): 21–34.

12. Grossman et al., "Turn Towards Practice."
13. Pam Grossman and Clarissa Thompson, "Learning from Curriculum Materials: Scaffolds for New Teachers?" *Teaching and Teacher Education* 24, no. 8 (2008): 2014–26; David Kauffman, Susan Moore Johnson, Susan M. Kardos, Edward Liu, and Heather G. Peske, "'Lost at Sea': New Teachers' Experiences with Curriculum and Assessment," *Teachers College Record* 104, no. 2 (2002): 273–300; Valencia et al., "Curriculum Materials."
14. David K. Cohen, Stephen W. Raudenbush, and Deborah Loewenberg Ball, "Resources, Instruction, and Research," *Educational Evaluation and Policy Analysis* 25, no. 2 (2003): 119–42; Heather C. Hill and Charalambos Y. Charalambous, "Teacher Knowledge, Curriculum Materials, and Quality of Instruction: Lessons Learned and Open Issues," *Journal of Curriculum Studies* 44, no. 4 (2012): 559–76; Remillard et al. (2009).
15. Joel D. Donna and Sarah R. Hick, "Developing Elementary Preservice Teacher Subject Matter Knowledge Through the Use of Educative Science Curriculum Materials," *Journal of Science Teacher Education* 28, no. 1 (2017): 92–110; Corey Drake, Tonia J. Land, and Andrew M. Tyminski, "Using Educative Curriculum Materials to Support the Development of Prospective Teachers' Knowledge," *Educational Researcher* 43, no. 3 (2014): 154–62; Cynthia C. Nicol and Sandra M. Crespo, "Learning to Teach with Mathematics Textbooks: How Preservice Teachers Interpret and Use Curriculum Materials," *Educational Studies in Mathematics* 62 (2006): 331–55.
16. Peter Youngs, Richard T. Holdgreve-Resendez, and Hong Qian, "The Role of Instructional Program Coherence in Beginning Elementary Teachers' Induction Experiences," *Elementary School Journal* 111, no. 3 (2011): 455–76.
17. See, e.g., Randi Nevins Stanulis, Sarah Little, and Erin Wibbens, "Intensive Mentoring That Contributes to Change in Beginning Elementary Teachers' Learning to Lead Classroom Discussions," *Teaching and Teacher Education* 28, no. 1 (2012): 32–43.

Chapter 5

1. Andrew J. Wayne and Peter Youngs, "Teacher Characteristics and Student Achievement Gains: A Review," *Review of Educational Research* 73, no. 1 (2003): 89–122.
2. Pamela L. Grossman, Sheila W. Valencia, Kate Evans, Clarissa Thompson, Susan Martin, and Nancy Place, "Transitions into Teaching: Learning to Teach Writing in Teacher Education and Beyond," *Journal of Literacy Research* 32, no. 4 (2000): 631–62; Jessica Thompson, Mark Windschitl, and Melissa Braaten, "Developing a Theory of Ambitious Early-Career Teacher Practice," *American Educational Research Journal* 50, no. 3 (2013): 574–615.
3. David K. Cohen, Stephen W. Raudenbush, and Deborah Loewenberg Ball, "Resources, Instruction, and Research," *Educational Evaluation and Policy Analysis*

25, no. 2 (2003): 119–42; Heather C. Hill and Charalambos Y. Charalambous, "Teacher Knowledge, Curriculum Materials, and Quality of Instruction: Lessons Learned and Open Issues," *Journal of Curriculum Studies* 44, no. 4 (2012): 559–76; Janine T. Remillard and Daniel J. Heck, "Conceptualizing the Curriculum Enactment Process in Mathematics Education," *ZDM, International Journal on Mathematics Education* 46 (2014): 705–18.

4. Joel D. Donna and Sarah R. Hick, "Developing Elementary Preservice Teacher Subject Matter Knowledge Through the Use of Educative Science Curriculum Materials," *Journal of Science Teacher Education* 28, no. 1 (2017): 92–110.
5. Corey Drake, Tonia J. Land, and Andrew M. Tyminski, "Using Educative Curriculum Materials to Support the Development of Prospective Teachers' Knowledge," *Educational Researcher* 43, no. 3 (2014): 154–62.
6. Ilana Seidel Horn and Britnie Delinger Kane, "Opportunities for Professional Learning in Mathematics Teacher Workgroup Conversations: Relationships to Instructional Expertise," *Journal of the Learning Sciences* 24, no. 3 (2015): 373–418.
7. Julie Cohen, "Challenges in Identifying High-Leverage Practices," *Teachers College Record* 117, no. 7 (2015): 1–41; Thomas J. Kane and Douglas O. Staiger, *Gathering Feedback for Teaching: Combining High-Quality Observations with Student Surveys and Achievement Gains*, MET Project research paper (Bill & Melinda Gates Foundation, 2012).
8. Peter Youngs, Lauren Molloy Elreda, Dorothea Anagnostopoulos, Julie Cohen, Corey Drake, and Spyros Konstantopoulos, "The Development of Ambitious Instruction: How Beginning Elementary Teachers' Preparation Experiences Are Associated with Their Mathematics and English Language Arts Instructional Practices," *Teaching and Teacher Education* 110 (2022): 103576.
9. Jillian M. Cavanna, Corey Drake, and Byungeun Pak, *Exploring Elementary Mathematics Teachers' Opportunities to Learn to Teach* (North American Chapter of the International Group for the Psychology of Mathematics Education, 2017); Casedy A. Thomas, "One University's Story on Teacher Preparation in Elementary Mathematics: Examining Opportunities to Learn," *Journal of Mathematics Teacher Education* 24, no. 6 (2021): 641–67.
10. Cohen, "Challenges"; Kane and Staiger, "Gathering Feedback."
11. David Blazar, "Effective Teaching in Elementary Mathematics: Identifying Classroom Practices That Support Student Achievement," *Economics of Education Review* 48 (2015): 16–29; Cohen, "Challenges."
12. Walter Doyle, "Ecological Approaches to Classroom Management," in *Handbook of Classroom Management*, ed. Carolyn M. Evertson and Carol S. Weinstein (Routledge, 2013), 107–36; David Stroupe, "Beginning Teachers' Use of Resources to Enact and Learn from Ambitious Instruction," *Cognition and Instruction* 34, no. 1 (2016): 51–77.

13. Helen Egeberg, Andrew McConney, and Anne Price, "Classroom Management and National Professional Standards for Teachers: A Review of the Literature on Theory and Practice," *Australian Journal of Teacher Education* 41, no. 7 (2016): 1–18, https://files.eric.ed.gov/fulltext/EJ1116396.pdf.
14. Dorothea Anagnostopoulos, Jillian Cavanna, and Sian Charles-Harris, "Managing to Teach Ambitiously in the First Year?" *Elementary School Journal* 120, no. 4 (2020): 667–91.
15. Grossman et al., "Transitions into Teaching."
16. Elham Kazemi, Hala Ghousseini, Adrian Cunard, and Angela Chan Turrou, "Getting Inside Rehearsals: Insights from Teacher Educators to Support Work on Complex Practice," *Journal of Teacher Education* 67, no. 1 (2016): 18–31.
17. Jonathan K. Foster, Matthew Korban, Peter Youngs, Ginger S. Watson, and Scott T. Acton, "Automatic Classification of Activities in Classroom Videos," *Computers and Education: Artificial Intelligence* 6 (2024): 100207; Jennifer Jacobs, Karla Scornavacco, Charis Harty, Abhijit Suresh, Vivian Lai, and Tamara Sumner, "Promoting Rich Discussions in Mathematics Classrooms: Using Personalized, Automated Feedback to Support Reflection and Instructional Change," *Teaching and Teacher Education* 112 (2022): 103631; Sean Kelly, Andrew M. Olney, Patrick Donnelly, Martin Nystrand, and Sidney K. D'Mello, "Automatically Measuring Question Authenticity in Real-World Classrooms," *Educational Researcher* 47, no. 7 (2018): 451–64.
18. Raj Chetty, John N. Friedman, and Jonah E. Rockoff, "The Long-Term Impacts of Teachers: Teacher Value-Added and Student Outcomes in Adulthood," Working Paper No. 17699 (National Bureau of Economic Research, 2011).

Methodological Appendix

1. Marilyn Cochran-Smith and Ana Maria Villegas, "Framing Teacher Preparation Research: An Overview of the Field," pt. 1, *Journal of Teacher Education* 66, no. 1 (2015): 7–20; Jenny DeMonte and Jane Coggshall, *New Collaborations, New Approaches: Research for Improvement in Teacher Preparation* (American Institutes for Research, 2018); Ashley LiBetti Mitchel and Melissa Steel King, *A New Agenda: Research to Build a Better Teacher Preparation Program* (Bellwether Education Partners, 2016); Christine Sleeter, "Toward Teacher Education Research That Informs Policy," *Educational Researcher* 43, no. 3 (2014): 146–53.
2. John W. Creswell and Vicki L. Plano Clark, *Designing and Conducting Mixed Methods Research* (Sage, 2017).
3. Peter Youngs, Lauren Molloy Elreda, Dorothea Anagnostopoulos, Julie Cohen, Corey Drake, and Spyros Konstantopoulos, "The Development of Ambitious Instruction: How Beginning Elementary Teachers' Preparation Experiences Are Associated with Their Mathematics and English Language Arts Instructional Practices," *Teaching and Teacher Education* 110 (2022): 103576.

4. Heather C. Hill, Brian Rowan, and Deborah Loewenberg Ball, "Effects of Teachers' Mathematical Knowledge for Teaching on Student Achievement," *American Educational Research Journal* 42, no. 2 (2005): 371–406.
5. National Mathematics Advisory Panel, *Foundations for Success: The Final Report of the National Mathematics Advisory Panel* (US Department of Education, 2008).
6. Joanne Carlisle, Ben Kelcey, Dan Berebitsky, and Geoffrey Phelps, "Embracing the Complexity of Instruction: A Study of the Effects of Teachers' Instruction on Students' Reading Comprehension," *Scientific Studies of Reading* 15, no. 5 (2011): 409–39.
7. Pam Grossman, Susanna Loeb, Julie Cohen, and James Wyckoff, "Measure for Measure: The Relationship Between Measures of Instructional Practice in Middle School English Language Arts and Teachers' Value-Added Scores," *American Journal of Education* 119, no. 3 (2013): 445–70.
8. Pam Grossman, Julie Cohen, Matthew Ronfeldt, and Lindsay Brown, "The Test Matters: The Relationship Between Classroom Observation Scores and Teacher Value Added on Multiple Types of Assessment," *Educational Researcher* 43, no. 6 (2014): 293–303; Thomas J. Kane and Douglas O. Staiger, *Gathering Feedback for Teaching: Combining High-Quality Observations with Student Surveys and Achievement Gains*, MET Project research paper (Bill & Melinda Gates Foundation, 2012).
9. Julie Cohen, "Challenges in Identifying High-Leverage Practices," *Teachers College Record* 117, no. 7 (2015): 1–41.
10. DeAnn Huinker, Cathery Yeh, and Anne Marie Marshall, *Catalyzing Change in Early Childhood and Elementary Mathematics: Initiating Critical Conversations* (National Council of Teachers of Mathematics, 2020); Steve Leinwand, *Principles to Actions: Ensuring Mathematical Success for All* (National Council of Teachers of Mathematics, 2014).
11. Matthew B. Miles, Michael Huberman, and Johnny Saldana, *Qualitative Data Analysis: A Methods Sourcebook*, 4th ed. (Sage, 2020).
12. Miles et al., *Qualitative Data Analysis*.
13. Miles et al., *Qualitative Data Analysis*.
14. Jillian M. Cavanna, Lauren Molloy Elreda, Peter Youngs, and James Pippin, "How Methods Instructors and Program Administrators Promote Teacher Education Program Coherence," *Journal of Teacher Education* 72, no. 1 (2021): 27–41.

Acknowledgments

We thank several individuals without whose engagement and support the Development of Ambitious Instruction (DAI) study and this book would not have been possible. First, we would like to express our gratitude to Pamela Grossman for giving us the opportunity to share the findings of our study in this book series. Pam's research on teacher education has long been a guiding light for us and for the field. Her development of the Protocol for Language Arts Observation (PLATO) and her groundbreaking work on teacher education pedagogies have been foundational to the DAI study. Second, we would like to acknowledge Fred Newmann's pioneering work conceptualizing and measuring ambitious instruction and his rigorous approach to qualitative case study research. Fred's high standards for classroom teaching and scholarship strongly influenced the DAI study.

We want to express our strong appreciation to the colleagues who worked with us as members of the DAI research team. Julie Cohen collaborated with us from the initial conception of this project through all aspects of the study. We especially benefited from her deep knowledge of PLATO and her focus on the complexity of how beginning teachers learn to teach and how we might capture such complexity in our analyses. Spyros Konstantopoulos, Kylie Anglin, Lauren Molloy Elreda, and Jason Miller played central roles in developing rigorous statistical models and carrying out the different quantitative analyses for the DAI study that we present in this book; we are indebted to each of them for their time, insights, and expertise. In addition, several doctoral students and postdoctoral researchers at University of Connecticut, Michigan

State University, and University of Virginia played crucial roles in collecting and analyzing classroom observation, interview, and survey data.

Our heartfelt thanks go out to the beginning teachers who graciously agreed to participate in the DAI study and allowed us to follow them as they took on the full responsibilities of teaching for the first time. We were consistently impressed by their commitment to fostering their students' learning and their willingness to share their successes and challenges with us. We are also deeply grateful for the openness, support, and insight provided to us by the directors, faculty members, cooperating teachers, and university supervisors with the five participating teacher preparation programs and the leaders, mentor teachers, instructional coaches, students, and parents in the schools and districts where the novice teacher study participants began teaching full-time. Conducting mid-scale, longitudinal research on beginning teachers' development of their instructional practices is truly a collaborative effort. We hope that the findings of the DAI study we present here will be as valuable to our partners in this research as their insights were to us.

The DAI study received funding from the National Science Foundation and the Spencer Foundation. We are grateful to the support we received from both organizations. The views we express in this book do not necessarily reflect the official policies or perspectives of these foundations.

Finally, we want to thank Karen Adler with Harvard Education Press for her careful editing and thoughtful feedback on chapter drafts. Her attention to substance and detail and her ongoing encouragement were invaluable.

About the Authors

Peter Youngs is a professor and Chair of the Department of Curriculum, Instruction, and Special Education at the University of Virginia. His research interests focus on how policies related to teacher preparation, induction, professional development, and evaluation are associated with beginning teachers' instructional practices, commitment, and retention. He currently leads a study of how neural networks can be used to automatically classify instructional activities in video recordings of elementary mathematics and language arts lessons and provide feedback to teachers on their instruction. He served as coeditor for *American Educational Research Journal* from 2019 through 2024.

Dorothea Anagnostopoulos is Professor of Curriculum and Instruction in the Neag School of Education at the University of Connecticut. She has extensive experience leading teacher education programs, including creating cross-institutional networks for improving teaching and teacher education and implementing practice-based teacher education reforms. Dr. Anagnostopoulos's research examines the sociocognitive, moral, and emotional work of teaching and teacher education. She is the lead editor of *The Infrastructure of Accountability: Data Use and the Transformation of American Education* (Harvard Education Press) and coauthor of *The Education Mayor: Improving America's Schools* (Georgetown University Press).

Jillian M. Cavanna is Assistant Professor of Elementary Education, STEM, and Innovation in the College of Education, Nursing, and Health Professions at University of Hartford. Her research focuses on mathematics education as well as teacher education more broadly. She examines how teachers understand and use data to justify and improve their teaching. Her research investigates the complex and overlapping contexts of the work of teaching and learning to teach. She is interested in research methodologies that honor and encourage the contributions of practicing teachers.

Corey Drake is Director of Professional Learning at The Math Learning Center, a nonprofit organization based in Oregon. Prior to joining The Math Learning Center, she was Professor of Teacher Education and Mathematics Education and Director of Teacher Preparation at Michigan State University. Her research is focused on the preparation and support of elementary teachers to teach mathematics to diverse groups of students in equitable ways. She has a specific interest in the role of curriculum materials in teachers' learning and practice.

Tutita M. Casa is Associate Professor in the Neag School of Education at the University of Connecticut, with expertise in elementary mathematics education. Her scholarship is focused on discourse, with an emphasis in writing. She is dedicated to creating and testing the impact of approaches advancing students' abilities to express their reasoning orally and in writing, reflecting ambitious mathematics teaching. She has published extensively for research and practitioner audiences, including in *Educational Leadership*, *Gifted Child Quarterly*, *Journal for Research in Mathematics Education*, *Journal of Writing Research*, *Mathematics Teacher*, *School Science and Mathematics*, *Teaching Children Mathematics*, and *Young Children*.

Index